Cover Photo

Tibet Himalaya

Nicholas Roerich

Copyright of the author J. Y. Kaheel

ISBN: 9798593227041

The Visitor

Transcendental Consciousness

J.Y. Kaheel

The Visitor

Transcendental Consciousness

To the Author

البحث عن الذات في خبايا اللاوعي الجماعي، مسار حياة في رحلات مريد: دار نلسون،
بيروت، 2012

دوائر روح متمردة: دار نلسون، بيروت، 2015

La Destination Incertaine, Serial of four Volumes :

1- Révélation d'un Papillon, [Create Space], Amazon, 2016

2- La Promesse, [Create Space], Amazon, 2016

3- Le Purgatoire, [Create Space], Amazon, 2016

4- Le Salut, [Create Space], Amazon, 2016

Dialogue avec mon Maître Intérieur, La Voie vers la Réalisation Mystique, [Create Space], Amazon, 2016

Epiphanie de l'Image Divine, Messages de Nulle Part, [Create Space], Amazon, 2016

À la Recherche de mes Racines, L'Enfant que J'étais, [Create Space], Amazon, 2017

La Destination Incertaine, Echos de ma Vie (Un Volume groupant la Série de quatre Volumes), [Create Space], Amazon, 2017

La Terre Change sa Peau, Vers un Nouvel Age [Create, Space], Amazon, 2017

[KDP, e-book], Amazon, 2018	إشارات الأزمنة،
[KDP, e-book], Amazon, 2018	فوق الإدراك،
[KDP, e-book], Amazon, 2018	الخرافة في العقل،
[KDP, e-book], Amazon, 2018	إلى الآلهة والى الأجداد
Amazon, [Create Space], 2018	الزائر،
Amazon, [Create Space], 2019	صوت الشلال
Amazon, KDP, 2019	To the Gods and to the Ancestors
Amazon, KDP, 2019	Above Perception
Amazon, KDP, 2019	The Myth in the Mind
Amazon, KDP, 2020	You are the Change
Amazon, KDP, 2020, eBook	الى الآلهة والى الأجداد، أنت هو التغيير
Amazon, KDP, 2020, eBook	كلمات في زمن الحرب، مأساة وطن
Amazon, KDP, 2020, eBook	منطقة الشفق، قمة المعرفة الباطنية
Amazon, KDP, 2020, eBook	طائر الحرية! هل يعود ؟
Amazon, KDP, 2019 VOL. II	To the Gods and to the Ancestors
Amazon, KDP, 2020, eBook	عارف أيوب الخوري، عتبة البتولية

Contents

Dedication

To my Sweetheart,
My wife, Alida, for the wonderful 50 years
We have shared and bear witness to the fact that you
are mine and I am all yours.

Thanks

I would like to thank
Miss Sara Haber for her efforts in making this
translation and presenting my book in
An English version.

Matthew 17:20 And Jesus said to them, Because of your unbelief. Indeed, I tell you, if you had faith like a mustard seed, you would say to this mountain, "Move from here to there, and so it moves, and nothing will be impossible for you."

Author's Word

I have been alerted since my youth that a Visitor has entered my consciousness and accompanied me in my travel and my departure. It was a presence of my great self, silent as the Sphinx, witnessing my practices, weighing them with the balance of the Divine Justice, enlightening my life, and offering me the wisdom of life. I followed the news of the wise men and the manner of their behavior and asceticism in this life, and their great silence. Moreover, once the circumstances put me in a bind, I would compete, even with my visitor, to get out victorious. The subject became in the hands of the universal mind, which began to inhabit, and I felt that I was constantly renewing, until I saw the light of the Golden Dawn emerge after my suffering, which lasted long. I felt it was my duty to be his spokesperson and his tongue. I began to see what cannot be seen, to hear the "sound of silence", to feel the hidden things, to follow the traces of the righteous without my knowledge, so I stopped spoiling the image with my thoughts, and I let life take the initiative, because I felt one with life. I never imagined them, but a state of revelation and enlightenment flooded me, such that I am no longer my old self, but I have been renewed by faith, piety, and love. A pure hand touched me, made me feel that I am a home to all the human values, and I am entrusted to them, and I am qualified to carry the torch. I walked silently and entered my hermitage proclaiming comfort, peace, and clarity of vision, because I transformed from form to the world of endless frequencies. This did not plunge me into the universe, but into the bosom of suffering humanity, which seeks salvation from poverty, ignorance, and hypocrisy. My happiness now lies in smiling eyes and hearts beating with love and peace. I became the Visitor, the Companion, and the Listener.

J.Y. Kaheel

1. VISION

The third eye, also called the eye of the mind, or the inner eye, is a mystical concept of the invisible, a contemplative eye that provides an awareness that transcends ordinary vision. They say that the third eye is the pineal gland. Ever since I was young, ideas and fantasies haunted me. Sometimes they would come to me during sleep, and sometimes during my meditation, and they would come without waiting, like a movie. A lot of light and wisdom frighten me, and I am not the righteous man who has never sinned. How can I bear these visions, which go beyond the reasonable, and take me to mazes, which are difficult to get out of? However, my soul has a safety valve, which guides me to the pathway, relieves me of my excessive irritation, and gives me the strength to endure, and the patience to understand the revelations, so they settle in my deep self, the prisoner of the Universal Order, which I observed closely.

I do not speak of what I have heard from others, nor from what I read in books, but from what I have seen, understood, compared, and checked for by myself, impartially, honestly, and faithfully, with some love and respect. However, I do not deny that I had an invisible partner; I felt his presence whenever I had to assess a situation. Come with me to our house behind the forest, where the silence and golden sun rays enter through the pine branches into the inner courtyard. Some chickens peck the earth, left and right, searching for their food throughout the day, and sheltering in their coop with the sunset. The wall clock, whose beats are heard from afar, also keeps in mind that, every evening, you must fill it with mechanical energy to rotate throughout the day, announcing the time, plus or minus five minutes, no difference! There are no beds in our house. However, some quilts and mattresses are scattered on the ground at night; and during the daytime, are kept in the "Lyouk", wall cupboard, covered by a sheet of cloth, walking on a metal wire tied with two screws that enter a wall of dried bricks made of mud and straw. In the guest room, there is a fireplace used to prevent the winter cold, with wooden windows from the outside for protection at night, and glass windows from the inside, allowing the light to enter during the day. There is a divan of high wooden seats, covered with cotton mattresses and straw cushions, and decorated cushions placed under the hand. In the corner of the room, there is a table with a radio that works on a battery and an antenna, and some old books for reading. In the middle of the room, there is an old picture of our ancestors hanging on the wall, and everyone who visited us would ask who was in the picture and say how beautiful it was.

When I was three years old, my father told me stories before going to sleep. My grandmother used to tell me, during the day, what she read from the stories of a thousand and one nights, and the stories of Girgi Zaydan, such as the Fatat (Girls) Ghassan, Armanosa of Egypt, the Virgin of Quraysh, and the Fatat (Girls) of Qairawan. My imagination's virility increased; I sailed in dreams far from reality, and felt a presence of another, listening to me, and guiding me to other joys of happiness and peace. As for my grandfather, he used to read a lot and give examples in every subject he came upon. Between my father Youssef and my grandfather Ayoub, I knew masculinity, the logic of life and discipline, and between my mother Alice and my grandmother Hannie, I knew femininity and compassion, and between myself and I, I knew awareness and wisdom.

Ever since my youth, I became aware that a Visitor had entered my unconsciousness and accompanied me in my journey and my departure. It was a presence of my Great Self, silent as the Sphinx, witnessing my practices, weighing them with the balance of divine justice, enlightening my life, and offering me the wisdom of life, in the form of lessons. Early on, I observed that life is not left to chance, but a self-governing system, and man can learn from the mistakes of others and the instinct of beings. He can learn administration from the ant's kingdom, pursuit and perfection from the bee's kingdom, piercing vision from the eagles, meekness from the lambs, and loyalty from the dog. Also, I began another quest, which is to explore the behavior of others in their life experiences, and then listen to the inner voice, and observe what the Visitor was showing me, while listening and learning lessons. What I understood at the age of five years changed as I grew up, as I turned ten and fifteen years of age. I would judge the appearance of things without knowing their essence; moreover, I would hasten in my judgments even if my information was incomplete, to impose my opinion on others. When I turned twenty years old, I began to wonder about the psychological reasons that drove people to act as they did. It got preoccupied with Freud's readings and his psychoanalysis. At the age of twenty-eight, came the role of reason and logic, and I began to put rules and laws in their proper context. All that I saw registered in my subconscious mind, but that did not protect me from the observations of others and the criticism of those who are more familiar with in life than me, so I pursued the news of the wise and the manner of their behavior and asceticism in this life and the abundance of their silence. It was assumed that this would teach me wisdom, but my preparations were not ready to endure, and I found myself needing meditation, isolation, and reflection. And if the circumstances put me in an impasse, I would compete, my Visitor and I, on how to emerge victorious. However, the emergent changes in my life changed the course of the goal, and it was not necessary to succeed or fail as much as it was necessary to maintain my psychological and mental balance to manage the rudder and guide the event to its happy conclusion. The issue became in the hands of the Universal Mind, which began to dwell in my heart, and I felt constantly renewed, until I saw the light of the Golden Dawn emerge after my suffering, which lasted long. I felt it was my duty to be his spokesperson and his tongue. I began to see what cannot be seen, to hear the "sound of silence", to feel the hidden things, to unknowingly follow the traces of the righteous, so I stopped spoiling the image with my thoughts, and let life take the initiative, because I felt I was one with life. I was never imagining, but a state of revelation and enlightenment flooded me. I am no longer my old self, but renewed by faith, piety, and love. A pure hand touched me, made me feel that I am a home to all human values and entrusted to them, and that I am qualified to carry the torch. I walked silently and entered my hermitage, preaching comfort, peace, and clarity of vision, because I transformed from form to the world of endless frequencies. This did not plunge me into the universe, but into the bosom of suffering humanity, which seeks salvation from poverty, ignorance, and hypocrisy. My happiness now lies in smiling eyes and in hearts that beat with love and peace. I became the Visitor, the companion, and the listener.

When we contemplate this vast universe, how the stars, suns, and planets rotate in the heavens, without colliding, how life on Earth came to be, and how it prospers, we would find that there is a rational creator behind all these systems, the Supreme Being. Here, the plant and animal kingdoms share among themselves and with the stars and planets, to maintain the equilibrium of the terrestrial environment. However, man has disobeyed, raped the laws of nature, and contributed in creating an imbalance with himself and the universe. So, wars, destruction, displacement, murder, and ruin were the scourges of human civilization. All this has developed, frighteningly, after the invention of the machine, the processes of manufacturing, and after man denied his relationship to Mother Nature, and destroyed it at times. Only at the beginning of this twenty-first century did civil society in the world feel the magnitude of the misfortune that humans have created in their environment. Therefore, associations were established that demanded that governments enact the laws that preserve the clean environment and ways to rebalance Mother Nature.

As for human society, we see a difference in the level of development of individuals, such that the wise advance the ignorant, and lead them to where they do not want, either through trickery, persuasion, control, injustice, or tyranny. However, whatever the means, people are free in what they choose and, in the end, they get what they deserve. Here, I do not search for divine justice and how to apply it as much as I search for the course of ordinary things that happen to individuals and groups. Therefore, my concern was to bring some of their behavior, and its consequences, and to stand on the most prominent results and provisions, and compare them to the so-called Karma in Hindu philosophy, or so-called divine justice in monotheistic religions, or fate and destiny in Islam. I found it useful to study how societies, cultures, and human personalities are formed, how they are affected by the environment in which they live, and by the climate of freedom or repression that prevails. Then there are the social phenomena, such as ethics, family, religious practices, and rules of professional conduct, which the individual accepts with all the obligations and coercion that they carry. There are also social currents that appear as waves of enthusiasm, gripping groups in casual conditions. All this has a strong relationship with the collective mind that dominates society. There is no doubt that there is a historical and temporal connection in one place, that is, a connection between the past and the present, in the form of phenomena and tendencies that existed in a period past. When these phenomena go beyond the humanly recognized boundaries, it is necessary to address these phenomena and consider them as subject to cause and effect. We must interpret the phenomena in the social milieu, the same one in which we live.

The phenomenon of **suicide** cannot be explained by purely psychological factors such as exposure to stress, fear and anxiety, but can be explained by social factors such as the failure of the individual in education, politics or love, or the exposure of his group to a disaster, or the ignition of a crisis in himself, or his isolation from society for some reason, which pushes some people to end their own life. It is necessary to adopt scientific methods to study these phenomena and how to treat them, and to neglect all metaphysical perceptions of the topic.

What we see today are social phenomena that are devoid of all accepted rules, regulations, and ethics. Which invites us to ask: to what extent did social institutions fail at maintaining the balance of their societies and distancing them from extremism?

Does what we read in the books about sociology, phenomena, and current social trends apply to the reality of the situation? Or was it hidden from Emile Durkheim and Ibn Khaldun, the excesses occurring in the world, which may threaten world peace and security, and take nations to confrontations like the two world wars, and the subsequent events of ethnic cleansing and the evacuation of minorities from their regions, under the guise of preserving their security and safety from infringements obtained from the majority opposed to them? Will there be an insight into avoiding the coming wars and re-establishing peace?

***

2. Rural Phenomena

The law of Karma is a moral concept found in the beliefs of Hindus, Buddhists, and other Eastern religions, which applies in a set of lives, while the law of causality applies in one life. "There is a cause for every effect", "what you sow, you reap", and there is no escape from the humanitarian duties that have been assigned to you in the past. Social heritage may feign ignorance and disconnection about past occurrences, such as the crushing of rights, by the unjust and tyrannical ruler. When you deny freedom to the group, and for a long time, submissiveness prevails in them, and they prefer to remain in their prison rather than explore the unknown and experiment with new means of development. This ignorance leads them to stubbornness, obstinacy, and pride in their behavior, and they misuse the machine, which goes with their lives; and the situations, which I experienced in the fifties of the twentieth century, in my village, Kfeir, were many:

Early death: I grew up with children who I used to go to school with and play with in the courtyards, and I have nice memories with them. One day, I received the news that Hamad had died in an accident while he was driving an agricultural tractor in the village. On another day, I received the news of Salman's death, for the same reason. Years later, I received the news of my friend Ziad's death, due to a traffic accident in Canada. Young people in the prime of life, forbidden to see them forever, and we do not know why it happened, but only how it happened. Of course, this has led me to wonder about the death of these young people; was it "fate and destiny", and I wanted to understand where the responsibility of those who had died has fallen, and where divine providence lies in all of this? Does it give up on us sometimes, and why? Alternatively, is it the law of causality, karma, or do we pay for our mistakes, and by it, we correct the path of another life, if found!

I remember, if someone died in my village, they would bring the body to a large tent in the public square, surrounded by a group of grieving women, and the men gathered around it and grieved in their way, especially if the deceased was young. The tunes of melancholy, the words of sadness and the crying still ring in my head, at every news of death from my village. It is one of the saddest voices that affects me, especially as it carries the echo of the absentee's qualities and his relationship with his loved ones and his family. These beautiful habits have become extinct long ago, overshadowed by forms of artificiality, shallowness, and emotion ceased among people and even among people of the same house.

Bad Emergence: From death we go to the rearing of children, in remote villages, where parents often poorly monitor them, so the child emerges as a plant between the thorns, and he may acquire bad qualities, if not challenged by parents. Whereas, in the absence of parents, the child, being an orphan, is raised by his relatives. The control may be non-existent, so the plant grows between the thorns, deviates from its proper behavior, and becomes a floating meal in the mouth of an intruder, a hungry animal, or an indifferent companion. Diseases come from all sides, and in the absence of necessary care, the plant gradually withers to dies on a cold winter night. My memories are sad for those who wandered around and roamed the streets to provide free services. He was lonely, orphaned, and homeless. Was it fate and destiny that this child lived homeless and died without caring for his condition, or was it the Divine Providence that wanted that?

Disability: Then there were in the village, strange cases of people whose physical and mental development stopped at a certain age, and rarely got out of their homes, and they would not go far. Even though I did not understand the meaning of these cases, I was nevertheless harsh in my judgments towards these children, because of my ignorance, my lack of culture, and my incomplete knowledge of life. One was older than me, and the other was my age. I would wonder, at length, about these people, and ponder: why are they so, perhaps it would have been if they were not born. I used to argue with them, knowingly, I was a child like them, and I did not hesitate to criticize and insult them, I even threw stones at them. Moreover, if I hit someone and hurt him, his mother would come frantically to my father to tell him. My father was on the lookout for my childish behavior, and he would immediately proceed to carry out the cruel punishment, which, according to him, I deserved. The punishments were: beating on the back with a pomegranate rod and kneeling for hours around a pillar of wood, in the "liwan", the center of the house. I got punished because of my bad behavior, but what about them? Are their cases a genetic consequence or a punishment for them and their families, for their misbehavior in previous lives, or has "fate and destiny" implemented its written judgments?

Madness: Then there was someone in an abnormal situation, and it was unreasonable for me, that is, the presence of a person, an elderly, with a white beard, who had a strange manner in dealing with others. It seemed to me that he did not allow anyone to touch him, not even members of his family. He walked away from pedestrians, and it appeared that in his walk, he chose every step away from the color white, and from the white line that we drew with chalk on the asphalt road, as a provocation. Nor did he leave the courtyard in front of his house. If necessary, he would go into his house, raise the lever handle with his elbow, and push the door with his feet, and as he entered, he would step away from the door and his wooden box so that his hands and clothes would not touch anything. I never saw him allow anyone, not even us young people, to approach him, though he would converse with us from afar. His behavior was an insurmountable issue, and according to me, it had no solution, and it formed a corner of reflection within my consciousness, not leaving its place for a moment, throughout the days of my life, until someone told me about his story.

Once, he went with his first wife to Mount Hermon, where it was covered with snow, and he killed her there. Then he married another girl from the village and had children. After a while, he lost his senses, perhaps he remained influenced by his crime, until he started distancing himself from people and even from his daughter, who sent him lunch every day, a jug of water, and a loaf of bread, which would feed him for a whole day. He did not get away with his crime in front of his living conscience. He suffered a psychological trauma that caused him to lose his mind and pay for his crime, a distorted and isolated life from the world. Was it an unpardonable punishment for a sin he committed when he was fully conscious, and did he harvest what he sowed?

Suicide: Whereas, the news of someone committing suicide, by shooting himself with a hunting gun, led my friends and me to go to see the victim, through a hole in the back door of the house. Consumed with terror of what would happen to us, from the man who ended his life with a shot. We could not see anything, only darkness, and absolute silence in the place. We wondered whether the ghost of the dead would remain near his body for a long time, in the place where he was killed, and whether it would hurt us if we smiled or laughed! His house was near the village cemetery, which made us panic more, us boys, and it was hard to get rid of the dark atmosphere that hangs over the dead and over our minds and senses. Fear of the dead did not prevent us, on hot summer days, from approaching the village cemetery, crossing over its boundary wall, to sit in the shade of the perennial oak tree. Moreover, some of the boys, who had an exaggerated curiosity, cruel hearts, and great courage, dared to walk among the graves and see the inside and what remained of the bones. However, as soon as the sun sets from the village and the darkness releases its shadows, we no longer dare to approach, except with someone older than us. As we passed by that place, we would hold his hand with great force, huddle ourselves along his steps, and talk about many things, so as not to feel the horror of the place, nor the perceptions that preyed on our psychological calm, which children usually enjoy.

I wondered then what prompted a wise man to end his life in a moment? Is it the harshness of life in the village and the obstruction of livelihoods, or the dark perceptions and psychological pessimism that have destroyed all hopes of life? Is suicide a voluntary act of free will? Does the person who committed suicide take responsibility for it? Alternatively, is it "fate and destiny" for some, or is it the abandonment of divine providence and leaving him before his painful end?

Custom: Generally, human society has developed from the family, to the clan, then to the tribe, the village, the city, the national society, and the liberal society. My village, Kfeir, is considered an advanced social component, on the path of civilization, because it is characterized by the social ethics of both the young and the old, in their daily lives, and it is seen as the cultural heritage of the grandparents, which transcends sectarianism and is inherited from generation to generation. Therefore, if someone behaved in a way we had not seen among people, we considered it outrageous behavior. Assaulting others' property and harvesting the fruit of their trees, borrowing from shops without paying what is required, misbehaving with others through lies and deceit, especially the treatment of the village girls and seducing them, are all heinous acts, accompanied by great criticism.

When death takes such cases, we wonder whether this was a "Fate and Destiny" or whether it was karma, or whether it was the divine providence giving up.

Fast enrichment: What about the ambitious young man, who emigrated to work for several years in the country of expatriation, to return home promptly with a fortune, which no one knows how he got it so quickly. As for his work, it was facilitated in the government departments; no one stood before him, and his relations with officials, old and young, were kept under wraps. Moreover, the viewer from afar says it might be the arms trade and brokerage, and another says maybe it might be the slave trade, and another says it might be the diamond trade, and another says it might be the drug trade. No one was able to reveal the identity of this prestigious figure, who was able to implement his dreams and found the fertile land for planting and harvesting his crops.

One day, I visited H. H., a friend of mine who, thanks to his intelligence, good performance, and gentle manners, worked with big construction companies in countries of the black gold. He told me how private planes were landing on the construction site where he worked, and emptied them under the cover of darkness. Perhaps it is the drug trade that has allowed the owners of these companies to become among the rich in the world, and the senior officials in their countries. Their ambitions were more than what was permitted, so they suffered from unrest and setbacks, but perhaps they changed their path. However, they pursued it under the influence of external pressures, but the final word came, ending their ambitions by surprise, during their bids, and left traces of confusion in the city.

Was it a "Fate and destiny", or the law of compensation and causality in which a person reaps what he sows, or is it the abandonment of the divine providence, so that he receives his inevitable end?

***

3. Mosaic Painting in Need of Restoration

Lebanese Politics: Let us return to the post-independence phase of the last seventy years of Lebanon's life. Since the populace, "Amiyet", of Antelias in 1943, and the storms ripple in the corners, with the influence of groups that consider themselves marginalized locally and from the regional, Arab, and international sides. Lebanon has known several security upheavals, including the revolution of 1958, the security movements inside and outside the Palestinian camps of 1969, and the civil war of April 1975, which lasted 15 years, and whose chapters have not yet ended. If the civil war has divided the Lebanese into warring sects, it has also destroyed decades of coexistence. It has also eliminated the face of justice, which Lebanon has known, through moderate figures. Hence, Lebanon began to move towards the unknown, and in its hand, a one-way ticket. The civil war has indeed ended, but at a great cost of debt to the Lebanese, which has now exceeded 80 billion US dollars. Therefore, the wheel of the economy did not move properly, and chaos spread in governmental administrations and institutions, corruption prevailed, and it has become impossible to push the state towards development and progress, unless there is a consensus between the political poles. The constitution was suspended, the term of the parliament's mandate was extended three times, and the position of presidency remained vacant for several years, until there was a regional, Arab, and international consensus on re-election. Moreover, now, there are many great and lingering problems. we hope that the current elected parliament will be able to renew the laws, boost the economy, stop waste and corruption, and solve the problems that have been lingering for years. Will they be allowed to do so? Nothing will change, "as long as" sectarianism, feudalism, and capitalism are in control, in the absence of respect for the Constitution and laws.

What will be the end of those individuals and groups who led Lebanon to this state of misery, under this programmed chaos, and at the advent of the New Age?

The Lebanese Civil War: I have noticed that the 1975 war has shown the stupidity of man, when the monster awoke in him. The Civil War exceeded the permissible and reasonable limits by committing crimes that are difficult to cover up, such as deliberate killing, forced kidnapping, violation of freedoms, burning of houses and properties, terrorizing the population and displacing them, and artillery and missile shelling. Fadi, who was affected by the war by one of those evil means and remained alive, was able to testify to the horrors of war, due to the physical deformities he carries to this day.

Was what happened what should have happened, or could it have been avoided, and how? Was what happened to those who were kidnapped, tortured, abused, and killed what should have happened to them, because of a divine will that holds everyone accountable, and no one can know how it is done? Moreover, for those who survived the punishment, was it because of the good deeds they had done in the past? Or did coincidence play its role, and those who killed, killed, and those who survived, survived! And if there is any responsibility, who should receive its consequences? Do we blame the heads of the militias, on the perpetrator of the heinous act, on the inherited system, on the sectarian formation in the country, or on those who assumed responsibility for the administration, the neighboring countries, and their blatant interference, or the alleged international conspiracy? When will fate (fate in the sense of what will happen) have its word in this, and will he give his verdict to those who committed massacres against their brothers? However, which fate are we talking about here? Should delusions take us the distance, when we lack the work of reason, logic, and wisdom, without knowing the real causes for war and the possibility of avoiding them? In addition, is there hope of reaching an enduring peace, with the existence of religions and doctrines that control the minds, souls, and homelands?

Corruption: As censorship waned during the last Lebanese Civil War, the administration worsened, bribes increased, and everything was bought with money, especially after the warring militias took control of many parts of the state, which led some to consider themselves as half-gods. Electricity, water, and telephone services seemed impossible, unless with an intermediary, which is either an intervention by a high-ranking official in a party or the state, or by paying bribes for the services. I observed these three things myself, and I suffered from two things. Moreover, if it wasn't for my good relations with some officials in the state, my home would have never received water, telephone, or electricity regularly, until recently. When the State regained some of its prestige and the militias and de facto forces ceased to control the lives of ordinary people, the situation returned to normal. However, that will not go without remembering what happened!

Those responsible for connecting the power lines found dead bodies on electricity poles, the water administrator died of a heart attack, and the official who was taking a thousand dollars in bribes, for the price of a phone line, was cut off from political life. Was it a "fate and destiny" or karma chasing them, or was it the abandonment of Divine Providence of those who renounced their living conscience for a handful of money? I am not saying that the situation now has been completely corrected, in terms of the electricity, because we now pay a state electricity bill and an electricity bill for the generator, which is twice as high. What happened was an implicit agreement between civil society organizations, municipalities, and generator owners, which is sharing the profits, the costs are on the citizen, and the state does not lift a finger. Moreover, we do not know how "Fate and Destiny" will deal with this general situation when all these organizations are involved in programmed thefts, especially in the absence of a long-term developmental project. I am not an expert on the subject; but I know that, they can use solar energy, especially since our country enjoys the sun most days of the year; or use wind to generate energy; or build new plants that can accommodate the energy required for at least 20 years with the possibility of expansion, which work on diesel or gas, by adhering to the countries that produce energy and do not deprive their people from it. Therefore, will they one day be charged for corruption and for using their positions for personal benefits, or by getting into the political scene, or being ruled by foreigners, because we are not worthy of being independent and free? Perhaps our presence as a small nation, with a range of ideological contradictions, will keep ablaze the differences between us, and we will not be able to dream of a strong civil Lebanon. If it is impossible to exclude sects from controlling state administration, we cannot reach a consensus agreement between blocs, parties, families, political poles, and sponsors of agreements, allowing the formation of Lebanon, a country with full sovereignty.

How can it be possible to remove Lebanon from the quagmire of sectarianism, if it is embedded in its demographic composition and if there are external threats affecting the structure of the society? Dream is something, and reality is another thing. The path of development is subject to social requirements and a strong will to adopt science to establish justice and equality among people, and not to blur religion as a useful social institution. The state is based on science, and religion is based on ethics, and one must not take the other's task. This is by excluding religion from the function of the state and vice versa. This solution may not achieve the secular dream, but it is a good step towards establishing rational thinking and separating the powers. Civil society, which has known civil wars every ten years, continues to groan under the results of the 1975 Lebanese civil war.

Arab revolutions and wars: What happened in Lebanon, stretched its sparks to reach all the countries from the ocean to the Gulf, and does not exclude anyone from a conspiracy under international auspices and undeclared aims to undermine what the ancestors planned, Fares and Fayez El Khoury, that is to establish secular states governed by laws, where citizenship rises above any religious, or sectarian affiliation. Does the displacement of millions from their homes and leaving them unprotected pour into what fate "wants" for those people? There are secret chambers of operations, which organize these absurd wars and promise the herds of men a better future. There is a scheme being implemented by human hands for certain undisclosed purposes. What we see and hear from international treaties indicates a continuous communication between rival groups and superpowers, that can impose peace, whenever they want, either by diplomacy or by iron and fire. Here appears the collective Karma, which forces people to pay for their ignorance and degeneration, until a leader is chosen for them, leading them to safety.

There is no doubt that we are living in a labor, because the circumstances in which we live after all these wars, and what accompanies it, from distorting the human image and the deterioration of social ethics, have left us with many questions about life and death, God, the universe, and man. We search for the status of each one of us according to our aspiration to exist as a conscious and responsible presence of humanity, most of whom still groan under the yoke of slavery, ignorance, poverty, neglect, homelessness, and loss. Humanity has lost its connection to its cultural heritage, and the civilization of consumption has brought it back to zero. The people have sought revolutions that overthrew tyranny, oppression, and defeat, but they were deprived of their freedom and independence due to new ideologies, led by slogans of humming ranting, and empty of content. People need to build the right citizenship in a clean geographical environment, suitable for the movements of other people. The goal behind establishing states is to realize the human dream, to benefit from the time in which he lives, and to seek the realization of the self, the goals that he deserves, his happiness, and his dreams.

However, people exist, each by their nature and cultural background, living within a specific geographical and societal framework, under a certain spiritual authority and another temporal authority, with a history spanning generations, and with a certain cultural heritage. Then, how can we help them understand their situation and the possibility of developing for the better, if we do not have the good will to truly help, understand the purposes, and have sublime goals of collectivism rather than division, peace rather than war, development rather than stagnation, and prosperity rather than poverty and hunger? It is the responsibility of all those who are aware of their position in this life to unite with their companions who share the same goals, to build a better future for all humankind. In addition to creating the appropriate climate to advance towards a united, free humanity, informed about its march towards the collective union and its proximity to the ideal picture of its existence.

***

4. Cultural Heritage and Its Preservation

Every creative work passes through three phases: 1 – The phase of mental preparation accompanied by a certain inspiration.

2 – The phase where the work is put into action.

3 – The phase of the period that passes before we arrive, and what accompanies it, from distortions of the original work. We can determine the environment that the creator grew up in, the time he lived in, the cultures he acquired, and how he is influenced by them. Every humanitarian action is subject to technical principles determined by specialists, according to its type and according to the development of psychology and aesthetics.

In the free world, intellectuals reject every superior thought that seeks control and indoctrination, brainwashing, perhaps because they absorbed the philosophy of the mind and called upon it to lead their life, away from religion. When work reaches a level of mastery, it is seen from two angles: the historical angle and the aesthetic angle, and it is evaluated according to its respect for these two characteristics. The advantage of a masterpiece is that it carries within it a cultural message for the emerging generations, and we must only preserve the authenticity of the masterpiece to carry out its mission. If distortions on it, the preservation and restoration process is based on a philosophical view of the past, which may vary from culture to culture. In countries that are subject to Islamic law, cultural heritage is the property of the endowments, and international initiatives cannot be taken to restore it, only by the Islamic vision. The distortion of antiquities in Afghanistan, Mali, Turkey, and other countries is only evidence of the intolerance of fundamentalist thought and its lack of appreciation for all that is contrary to its beliefs. In addition, the wars that have been sweeping the Middle East are just another example of the sectarian conflicts that have not been extinguished for hundreds of years.

Perhaps our religious view of the past and our attachment to it as the highest level of enlightenment that we can reach, because it's the era of the prophets, has frozen every free human development and handed the leadership over to the religious texts and their irrational interpretations. Over a few hundred years, Europe has managed to separate religion from politics and rationalize the laws of the states. However, it was not the appropriate solution, because we see a delinquency in society towards atheism, which began to neglect religion, prayer, charity work, and the societal spirit on which it grew up. Suicide increased in the more developed countries, reproduction decreased to below the required level, and the population began to decline as if Europe would disappear from the map in thirty-nine years! As the number of new expats and immigrants from Third World countries increases, due to social contributions and aid, Europe will be full of residents from Africa, the Middle East, and the Far East. Moreover, if no change occurs in the situation in general, then the European culture is on the path to extinction!

Was this due to disconnection with the cultural heritage or from not restraining consumer materialism and limitless freedoms, or is this the year of development, and everything develops at the expense of something else? Is what is adopted by the Islamic peoples in terms of breeding offspring and living in poverty, a guarantee to ward off the danger and guarantee the continuity of the development of their culture? I believe that man should be free and responsible in choosing what he wants, and God is aware of everything we do, and at the same time, "He does not change what people do, until they change what they do themselves". Surah Al–Raad

***

5. Fate and Destiny

It may be useful to draw a comparison between the beliefs of religions and doctrines to understand "Fate and Destiny", due to the importance of its influence on collective behavior, and to compare it with the law of Karma and the law of causality.

In the law of the Torah, the Jews make mistakes, and they take responsibility for their errors. God forgives them for the sake of their father Abraham or Jacob, for the sake of Moses or David, but they are the ones who make mistakes, and God does not appreciate their actions and deeds.

In Christianity, there is confusion between some verses from the Old Testament and the New Testament. Some verses speak of "Fate and Destiny": "Before the creation of the universe, He knew everything" Bin Sirach 20:23. Because God already knew what they would do. "And in your books, you have written all my days, and have pictured them, before they were anything." Psalm 139/16. However, some verses contradict the idea of "Fate and Destiny": "and if you do not listen to the words of my servants the prophets, whom I sent repeatedly (though you have not listened)" Jeremiah 26/5. "Honor your father and mother, so that your days may be long in the land that the LORD your God is giving you" Exodus 20/12. "Who are those who fear the LORD? He will show them the path they should choose" Psalm 25/12. "A person's decision leads to one of those consequences: good or evil, life or death" Bin Sirach 17/ 3-18. "Repent, for the kingdom of the heavens is near" Matthew 4/17." He that is without sin among you, let him first cast a stone at her" John 8/7. Jesus says in the Bible: "A hair from your head will not fall except with the knowledge of your Father, who is in the heavens", and he doesn't say by the will of your Father! There is a great difference between knowledge and will. If, on the contrary, I say "by the will of your Father", here, I make God responsible for the fall of the hair, and this thought is the peak of **Fatalism**. The Bible proves to us that there is no place for "fate and destiny" in the Christian faith. We put, in its place, the concept of "Divine Providence," which is not Fatalism. When God created us, he put in us a continuous capacity for creation and creativity.

In Islam, the concept of "Fate and Destiny" is an overriding concept in the Quran, which cannot be disputed. In every Surah, perhaps in each verse, you notice and feel that God has judged, determined, and defined ... This concept, if it is understood literally, may stop a Muslim's mind, because God wrote everything. These are the views of some Islamic sects:

Qadariyah is an originally derogatory term designating early Islamic theologians who asserted that humans possess free will, whose exercise makes them responsible for their actions, justifying divine punishment and absolving God of responsibility for evil in the world. The term derives from قدر (*qadar*), "power". Some of their doctrines were later adopted by the Mu'tazila and rejected by the Ash'aris." Others among them believe that God is aware of people's actions but denies their occurrence by the will of God, His power, and His creation, which is the basis of their doctrine. In addition, these proved a Creator with God.

In opposition is **Determinism** (الجبرية) who exaggerate in proving fate, that they even deny that there is, for the person (the slave), an act of reality. Rather, according to them, he has no freedom, no choice, no action. Like a feather in the wind, his acts are metaphorically assigned to him, **so they say: pray, fast, kill, and steal.** It is also said: the sun rose, the wind blew, and the rain poured. They accused their Lord of injustice and entrusting people (the slave) with what they could not do and rewarded them for what is not from their doing. They accused Him of tampering with the assigned servants and nullified the wisdom of command and the prohibition. This implies that the person (the slave) is not to blame for his transgressions and sins. It is no secret that what is in this statement causes a clash with the provisions of the Sharia, which leads to corruption.

As for **the Sunnah**, they believe that God knew things before they were, that He estimated the sources of everything before Creation, and whatever He wanted was, and whatever He did not want was not, and that He is the Creator of all things. In addition, people are free – universally - in assigned acts, they are not forced to disobedience or obedience, they are truly active, and God is the creator of their actions. "**Shifa Al Alil**, Healing of the Sick in matters of fate and destiny, wisdom and reasoning," **Ibn Qayyim al-Jawziyya**

Murji'ah (Arabic: المرجئة, "Those Who Postpone"), also **Murji'as**, **Murjites** or **Murji'ites**, is an early Islamic sect. Murji'ah held the opinion that God alone has the right to judge whether a Muslim or not has become an apostate. Consequently, Muslims should practice postponement (*ìrjā*) of judgment on committers of major sins and not make charges of disbelief (*'takfir'*) or punish accordingly anyone who has professed Islam to be their faith. The school is now considered extinct – Wikipedia. They base their belief on the almighty saying (interpretation of the meaning): "Those who are guided by the command of Allah will either be tortured or atoned for. Allah is All-Knowing and wise." Verse 106: **Surah Al-Tawbah,** (repentance) and their basic tenet is not to atone to any person, whomever, if he converted to Islam, and uttered the two Declarations of Faith, whatever sins he has committed, leaving the decision to God alone. So, they used to say: disobedience does not harm faith, just as obedience does not benefit infidelity." Wikipedia

Reconsidering the reading of the Quranic text: The goal of delving into this delicate subject is a modest attempt to reach a restoration of the image that comes to us, due to a misunderstanding, from reading the Quranic text. Everyone knows that the Holy Quran is considered the descended word of God. It is the divine constitution after which God sealed the books, completed the religion, and accomplished grace on the Muslims. Some say no to interpretation, and others accept interpretation. I am not familiar with the issues of the Islamic religion until I became able to interpret what the intellects couldn't, but my goal is not to criticize the concept of the text nor interpret it, but to re-read it and fear God Almighty. The first verse begins with the word "read," and the last verse begins with the word "and fear (piety)", and this is what I am doing.

It is useful to know the historical sequence of the modern reading projects of the Quranic text, which began with Orientalism. In 1312, the Synod of Vienna adopted the ideas of **Roger Bacon** and approved the teaching of the Arabic language in five European universities - the universities of Paris, Oxford, Bologna, Salamanca, and the city of the Papal city of Kurie.

In the year 1539 AD, the first chair for the Arabic language was established in the Collège de France in Paris. This chair was occupied by **Guillaume Postel**, the first orientalist, who said: "No one can reject the remedies of Arab medicine. Ibn Sina (Avicenna) says in one or two pages more than Galen says in five or six large volumes". http://elibrary.mediu.edu.my/books/SDL0512.pdf.

Some may find that the orientalists have caused despair in the future, abhorrence of the present, and mistrust of the past. Modern intellectual projects of reading religious texts are in response to the cultural challenge imposed by the clash with Western civilization, with its intellectual, societal, and political ideas and products. This appears in three phases:

The first phase started in the late 19th century and the beginning of the 20th century, with the fall of the Arab civilization and its backwardness. Then began the attempts of scholars and intellectuals to re-read the Arab and Islamic heritage; to try to find out the cause of decadence and backwardness; and to put forward intellectual projects to advance the nation, and to break away from the bonds of Western civilization. Thus, **Mohamed Abduh**, **Jamal al-Din al-Afghani**, and **Rifa'a al-Tahtawi** made their attempts to reconcile the legal text and some Western intellectual products.

The second phase appears in the early fifties of the twentieth century; the methodology of reading the religious text using modern methods appeared in the readings of **Taha Hussein**, **Amin al-Khuli,** and **Muhammad Ahmad Khalaf Allah**, using in their readings of these stories, the mechanisms of the historical human mind.

The third phase: In the late 1960s and after the Arab setback in 1967, the third wave began, with many Arab intellectuals turning to re-read the heritage with a complex of Western superiority, and exposing the Arab inability to fill the gap of cultural inequality, which hurt the Arab personality, taking the form of "collective neurosis," according to **George Tarabichi**. This phenomenon consists of several streams, including what was read on the banks of the religious text, such as **Al-Jabiri**, **Al-Arawi**, **Hussein Mroueh,** and **George Tarabichi**. Among them are streams within the program of circulation, such as **Gamal al-Banna** and **Mohammed al-Ashmawi**, and their readings did not derive their mechanisms from outside the scope of Islamic deliberation, for diligence in relying on modern methods. Among them was **Mohamed Arkoun**, and his methodology for reading the Quran text includes a historical critical reading according to the linguistic, semantic, and analytical approach of the Quran. He has published it in his book: "The Qur'an from an inherited interpretation to an analysis of religious discourse" to present its true meanings and to invalidate its inherited interpretations, but to highlight the linguistic and semantic qualities, the mechanisms of presentation, independence, persuasion, and communication and the moral purposes of what he called the prophetic discourse. Including **Abdul Majid al-Sharafi**, who relies on the results of the new curriculum for the study of religion, humanity, language, and history. In addition to **Hassan Hanafi**, who presents an astonishing example of the duality of the Arab mind in its oscillation between the poles of heritage and modernity, and in its schizophrenic confusion between two cultural strategies: self-criticism and self-inflation. He says, "... God is but the awareness of the human to himself and his qualities and names are nothing but human hopes and the goals that they aspire to. Also, secularism is the basis of revelation, and religion is an expression of history-making, which appears in moments of societal backwardness and stops it from developing. Heritage is a national issue and not a religious one.

Including **Nasr Hamid Abu Zayd**, the creator of the intellectual project in re-reading the religious text, as a historical reading. The Qur'an, according to him, contains many verses that are difficult to conform to international standards of modern democracy and human rights. Historical in the sense that to considers the religious texts as cultural production governed by the social, cultural, and political field of society according to its historical and geographical conditions. The divine source does not exclude it from these laws because it has been humanized since it was embodied in history and language. The texts are fixed in pronunciation, variable, and changing in concept. He refuses "to be seen" as a slave to God, and he steadfastly refuses to live in vain with a set of constants.

Including **Adonis Ali Ahmed Said**, his method includes re-reading the Quranic text, because extremism is based on a special and violent interpretation of religion, he dreams of restoring the Caliphate. He presents a bad and hostile image not only of civilization and culture, but also of man. Regarding the religious text exclusively, there is no sense in modernity. True religious reform is the separation of religion and politics.

Perhaps reality is the best proof of what the Arab and Islamic countries suffer in the present time, from confusion and setbacks in their social conditions, and the wars they are suffering from. Perhaps like Malaysia, **Mahathir Mohamad** is the best, to know how to deal with religion in a civil state and not a secular state.

***

6. The Need for Modernity

It is the habit of the Visitor to listen, look, contemplate, and highlight what he sees, then go on his way. He neither asks nor gives, neither loves nor hates, neither clings nor separates; he is like the light that comes from afar to lighten our consciousness. This Visitor has lived inside me, he has seen through my eyes, has heard through my ears, and desires to stay with me, because my mirror reflects the reality of my feelings towards man and the universe.

What worries me is reading the reality of the society to which I belong, wondering how to better understand what is happening, and whether I can shed light on all the dark corners so that the emerging generations can take responsibility for their future. What caught my attention is the existence of destructive social phenomena, and we must search for what they are, how they are formed, and the extent of their ability to change. Social phenomenon is the different types of behavior and thought patterns that are characterized by being beyond one's control, but rather are received from the society they grew up. It is manifested in the fact that it imposes itself on the individual in society without realizing it. The social phenomenon emerges from the action and the reaction between the conscience and the mind, as it does not arise from the actions of individuals but from the inspiration of the mind and the making of society. It results from several psychological, religious, economic, and other factors. Therefore, man is subject to the influences of the society in which he grows and lives without his knowledge, and this is dangerous. As such, this reality shows how much the individual must work to gain complete freedom to choose what he wants.

Man is a being alien to all other creatures, as he rationalizes, understands, chooses, and searches for the truth. It cannot be chance that governs his fate, because he is not born of chance, but rather is born of a comprehensive cosmic system, looking for a role model in the perfection of existence. The most important thing that can be offered to him is to secure his innate freedom before his knowledge overwhelms it. We need intuition on the one hand and awareness and the power of reason on the other. Simple religious concepts uttered by revelation and science utter everything that does not conflict with the merit of consciousness and the power of reason. The issue is to provide the necessary position so that thought does not die and that political transformations do not take place, which leads to the rise of extremism and wars. Before delving into this topic, we must draw a framework for the development of understanding in man, which is based on his knowledge of himself and his entity, so that he can recognize the inseparable presence of human consciousness.

Paul Ricoeur says: **"The human understanding of himself and the world around him is based on the language that expresses this understanding"**. **As for Heidegger**, he considers language to be the main capacity of man, which grants him his humanity, by the contents, implications, and meanings of the human mental dimensions that distinguish him from other beings. Eventually, speech does not mean anything but an attempt to agree on the symbols, and monitor their implications, to achieve mutual trust about the symbols spoken about. We live in this world with others, and some have a constant tendency toward transcendence and detachment from others. Man is the one who makes existence meaningful by his rational and wise readiness in the present, and does not accept any external aid to determine his authenticity and the reality of his existence.

In this world, no one can persist and develop alone, without the need for what and who surrounds them. His presence among his peers requires him to extend his hand and constructively cooperate with them and to show them all the knowledge and credibility in dealing, and to remove all thoughts of arrogance and paradox that keep him away from others. What we apply to the individual must be applied to human societies, because their purpose in life must be to bring goodness, happiness, and peace to other societies.

Modernist movements have begun to develop and liberate societies, but they have fallen into the trap of the tyranny of the mind, the decline of the spirit, the confusion of the human being, and the confiscation of their abilities. With the wars and changes taking place in the world, the dreams of modernity collapsed, and ideological currents emerged that rejected and rebelled against the myth of the self, and criticized the overall logic in politics, morals, and the authoritarian regimes that followed it, and opposed all thinking fortified with the illusion of certain knowledge. Modernity gave up its monetary power and hurt the mind to serve the authority and capitalism.

Among these currents was existentialism, which went directly to the living, existing man and not to the human being in the absolute. Existence is not absolute, stripped of its sensory and mental content. Speaking of existence does not mean talking about what is. Therefore, the confusion between the universe and being goes to nihilism that aims at controlling man. If we think about the universe, we must think about the existing beings in which the universe is manifested, including man, the only being who has a permanent relationship with himself, that is, he has the property of being. The human being is distinguished by the immediate, a property that reduces the personality to the present instant. The immediate is embraced in heritage, customs, and history in general. It is necessary to remove the blockages that have accumulated on the heritage and return to the sources of concepts and statements that have been distorted by the successive doctrines that have neglected the main question of existence.

A person, whatever his belief, cannot escape from the truth of himself, his cultural heritage, and his duties towards his person, his society, and humanity. The space of freedom given to him is the only outlet that he must use to keep his mind and heart working for his good. He is first and foremost responsible for developing his character and its encounter with the ideals and values he believes in. Everything changes in this universe, and the perspective of man changes according to his level of cultural and aesthetic understanding of life and the development of psychology. He is the one who must paddle to get his boat to safety, given the circumstances available to him that may help him overcome obstacles. All there is, is a leap of faith, self-confidence in the self, and the perfect human being who carries his image, to get out of the dilemma which life wants to put him in! It is a story of consciousness that transcends the whole, stripped of every guardianship and narrow-mindedness, and every shell or prejudice to any side. Returning to instinct and to what it carries in the spontaneity of expression helps man remove the clouds of conservatism, and to have a clear vision of himself and the world. It remains for him to have the courage to take the initiative and to see himself as a being in which the universe is manifested. He must not underestimate the value of his heritage to appear in tune with his time, but rather he must revive it by his new view of man and the universe, through **pantheism**. That unity that does not set conditions on anyone to belong to it, because it lives in every part of this universe. The world is collapsing before disintegration, and what is required is a new formulation of its unity; perhaps the spread of education, science, and culture is what is needed.

***

7. Character and Personality

If we look scientifically at humans, we see that genes play a role in their behavior, in harmony with the environment. Social, economic, and political conditions play a major role in stimulating or inhibiting the genes that control violence, anger, depression, and others. However, the differences between individuals, in terms of intensity or weakness, may be due to the circumstances they face, the force of excitement, or both, and the readiness of the individual to withstand these conditions. The genes of the brain cells, through their secretions, play a key role in human behavior. The scarcity or multiplicity of its secretions depends on the effectiveness of the existing gene and its interaction with the environment. Therefore, the response of individuals who live in different countries towards similar events would be dissimilar, due to the behavior of the genes affected by the environment. I do not think that the nature of the subject to genes can be reduced to a person materially, for there is will, awareness, freedom of action, intuition, sublimation, and everything that guarantees freedom of choice. Every human being can acquire and adapt their behavior and personality, independent of biological determinism. To identify behavior, we remain detached from the complex understanding of gene interaction with acquired experiences. No one teaches the human being how to laugh or how to cry because these are innate signs used by everyone. Moreover, no one teaches the bees how to harvest honey from flowers, because bees are born equipped with a variety of programs that help them complete their work. There is an ecological balance in nature, in the plant kingdom as well as in the animal kingdom, as if it has its reasons to avoid the escalation of fighting between them, which might harm it and harm their relations. As if animal behavior evolves according to the benefits that they derive individually. Although ant soldiers sacrifice their lives in defense of their colonies, and dolphins lift their companions to the surface of the water to supervise their drowning. In the case of two unrelated animals, the assistance they provide to each other must be reciprocated later. These behaviors are somewhat like human behavior in a human society based on the same perspective of family values and economic equivalence.

Some human behaviors can be changed easily because it is the result of learning and acquisition, while others resist change because they are part of the biological inheritance. Some people, unlike social insects, generally attend to their interests before the interests of their community, while others not only cooperate but also sacrifice themselves for the sake of the whole. The ideology of the elected elite that spread in Germany was preceded by the eugenics movement that spread among the thinkers of the United States and Britain. The capitalist economy and the lack of government intervention, in which the strong remove the weak from competition, leading to an improvement in the situation of the population, in general, affect the political programs. So, they do not help the poor in their struggle to survive so as not to break the natural order, and this is the tragedy. There is nothing that politics has entered without spoiling it. Science awaits the results of recent discoveries and experiments to see how genes and cognitive gains affect human behavior. Thus, it is easier to help societies emerge from their shell to enter the new world.

***

8. Closed Worlds

In this closed and limited world with its personalities, events, and interactions, everything that happens to us is a cause or a result of what others have done, even if it may seem that we are the ones who did it. All the fluctuations that have occurred on earth since the dawn of history, can be reduced to graphics that show us the details of what happened at the time and place, whether on the geographical, populace, war, or religious levels, to the events that have passed and changed the face of the earth. With the development of science in general, everything is now under the microscope, and what was said to be inaccessible has become accessible to the scientific researcher, because of the fruitful cooperation between parties of specialized institutes, for the ease of communication between them, and for the credibility that they have.

There are closed worlds in all human activities, from literature to thought, philosophy, science, religion, etc., all of which are subject to a certain structure that maintains its continuity. Moreover, the most complex are religions, because they involve the unseen in their structure, so that no researcher can delve into their beliefs without destroying a large part of them, and this is not required, in my opinion, as long as they perform their positive function in human society.

True creativity, in its essence, is a spiritual experience, closed to the perceptions of sensation, visualization, and science. This creativity appears in literature, poetry, and the arts, such as theater and music, but it is distinguished by the phenomenon of mysticism. The West has been interested in Islamic mysticism and spiritual and esoteric teachings since the Renaissance, and has continued to this day. In the eighteenth century, an orientalist Sufi movement emerged that managed to crystallize the features of the Romantic school, which spoke of the paranormal (from the mystical point of view) and dignities, and confined its interest to humans and to the upper worlds where the angels are. This resulted in a contemplative theory with an oriental epistemological philosophy that glorifies nature and calls for a return to it. Here, people stop dreaming of a revolution to change the world, and start thinking of a revolution to change the self. However, the soul has valleys and labyrinths, and contains secrets and riddles which are difficult to detect, especially if you enter into a mystical experience. The rationalist, no matter how knowledgeable or far–sighted he is, remains incapable of obtaining the spiritual knowledge that the disciple obtains. The reason is the unwillingness of the soul to accept metaphysical knowledge, which is not subject to the scientific-analytical method, but rather to spiritual revelation by inspiration and intuition.

Ibn Arabi says that he purified himself before his ascension to heaven, so that he would get rid of all his ills, represented by his corrupt elements of water, dust, air, and fire. Then he began his journey through the seven heavens, to reach the end of "Sudrat Al-Muntaha", where he "the lights covered him until he became all light and took off a dress, that he had never seen anything like", to complete his path. He tries to show how to reach the sanctuaries of revelation, and language cannot express what cannot be described, even if it uses poetry. When poetry reaches its climax, language verges on breaking down and loses its role in front of what appears to the seeker, so it turns into signs and symbols that appear only to those who have reached the highest levels of revelation, because what is seen by the seeker exceeds every description. This world is closed off to all knowledge.

9. One Thousand and One Nights

"It is a book that includes a collection of stories that occurred in Western and South Asia, as well as folk tales that were collected and translated into Arabic during the golden age of Islam. The book is known as the Arabian Nights in the English language since its first edition, which was issued in 1706. For centuries, authors, translators, and researchers from West, Central, and South Asia and North Africa compiled the work of the book. The tales date back to the ancient and medieval centuries of the Arab, Persian, Indian, Egyptian, and Mesopotamian civilizations. Most tales were originally popular stories from the Caliphate Period, whereas the rest, especially the story of the frame, were probably derived from the Persian pagan work "Thousand Myths", which in turn was partly based on Indian literature. While some say that the origin of these novels is Babylonian. The main frame story of "One

Thousand and One Nights" narrates the story of a king called Shahryar. Shahryar discovers that his brother's wife was a traitor, which shocks him. What made matters worse was his discovery of his wife's betrayal of him, too, which was unbearable for him, so he decided to execute her, and saw that all the women were wrong. Daily, the king married virgins and killed the bride on their wedding night, so as not to take the opportunity to betray him. After a while, the minister, who was tasked to provide a bride to the king, found no more virgins. Then, his daughter Shahrazad offered herself as a bride for the king, and her father reluctantly agreed. On the night of their wedding, Shahrazad began telling the king a story, until the coming morning came and she became silent, promising the king that she would complete the story the next night. This incited the King's curiosity to hear the end of the story, prompting him to postpone her execution. The next night, when she finished telling the story, she would start a new one, causing the king to yearn to hear its end, and so on, until she completed a thousand and one nights.

There are some famous stories in the book "One Thousand and One Nights", such as "Aladdin and the Magic Lamp", "Ali Baba and the Forty Thieves", "The Seven Voyages of Sinbad", and other folk tales. Some say that Shahrazad asked for amnesty, while others mention that when King Shahryar saw their children, he would decide not to execute her, while some versions talk about the king's confusion and one result, which was amnesty for Shahrazad and stopping his habit of killing women." Wikipedia

The French Antoine Galland (1646-1715) for the first time translated some of these tales into French, and its first edition appeared in the years 1703 and 1717, which caused an uproar in the aristocratic circles. Years later, the East became a source of inspiration for Western writers, poets, and artists, either because of their curiosity to know these closed worlds, or to look for something they lacked; self-exploration could be through others. The unbridled imagination of the unknown shows how to create hope and give the oppressed a chance to get out of prison to the horizon of freedom. Every story in "One Thousand and One Nights" resembles the expanse of light and hope in which Shahrazad lives. Thus, a person lives, every night, a space of hope that grows and shortens according to the breath of his perceptions and his fertile imagination.

***

10. Imagination and Creativity

The Westerners were impressed by the strength of symbolism and imagination of the Sufi texts. For example, the story of "Majnoon Laila" was distinguished by its symbolism, where the female symbolizes the soul that seeks the highest or the absolute. There is no creativity without imagination, and there is no imagination without a symbol that draws it to its closed worlds. The mystical text is known for its freedom in performance, in breaking the familiar and embracing the absolute, blowing up language and sending it with maximum energy to give it the ability to deliver that astonishment, but the imagination is like a horse without a bridle; it can take its knight nowhere, to his end. It is true that we need imagination to distance ourselves from boredom and poverty, to live our lives with hope. However, we also need ways to understand reality and work to overcome difficulties, and this is done only by setting a scientific standard for our actions. This is the first time we have lived on earth, unable to remember past lives, although our genes record all our physical and psychological abilities. Everyone is thirsty for life, with the hope that it lasts forever. Several thousand years ago, religions came to lay down their beliefs as a reference for their followers on life and death, God, and the universe. In addition, they considered the arrival of their prophets and the moment of their departure as a beacon of the best and most beautiful in existence, where time ceases with them. There is no value in existence in the time before their presence, and the universe after them declines towards its end. History has stopped at that moment, this is how fundamentalists see life, although it is completely different from what science has discovered after painstaking research and tremendous progress in the concepts and methods adopted.

"Science has reached a measure of the age of the Earth of about 4.54 billion years, and the age of the sun of about 4.57 billion years, that is, the sun is thirty million years older than the Earth. As for the human being, the only remaining organism of the Homo sapiens, a branch of the hominin tribe, who belongs to the family of the great apes is the only one who is sane, who, unlike the rest of the animals on Earth, has a highly developed brain capable of abstract thinking, the use of language, speech, internal self-reflection, and solutions to the problems faced by man. Not only that, but humans have an erect body with upper and lower articulated limbs, easy to move and operate in full harmony with the brain. This property makes man the only living organism on earth capable of employing his mental and physical abilities to make accurate and inaccurate instruments that he needs in his daily life. Fossil studies and analysis of mitochondrial DNA have revealed evidence indicating that modern humans were in Africa about 300 thousand years ago. The Sumerian civilization in Iraq is considered one of the oldest civilizations from 5300 to 2000 BC. Wikipedia

Religion is based on the unseen and revelation, and science is based on experience and abstract concepts, and they do not converge on the concept of life, the universe, and man. The danger in the religious view is denying the historical character of the human being and suspending him in metaphysical molds. The danger in the scientific view is in ignoring the imagination and preconceived sense, and in not giving man hope in another life after death.

***

11. The Pilgrimage between the Visible and the Invisible

In the Bible, in the Old Testament, there is an analogy between the human being, the visible one, and God, the inner and invisible one, which led Jewish philosophers to interpret. Therefore, their work on the creation of an idea of God is summarized, which transcends the senses, by their interpretation of the texts, which is understood as an analogy between God and man. This means that there is a dynamic of faith in the Torah, behind which lies an inner dynamic, that is, Greek philosophy. As such, both dynamics act like two poles, one apparent and the other mystical. That is, the Torah has two meanings, one literal and the other metaphorical. Greek philosophy was the foundation, and the Torah represents mysteries and contemplation. Only through interpretation can we understand its metaphorical meaning. Here, symbols have entered the world of ideals and basic qualities such as mind, sense, soul, pleasure, pride, goodness, sun, moon, and earth.

In the Bible, in the New Testament, Jesus' words were like distant projections on the minds of his disciples, and like symbols of obedience, virtue, love, and poverty that call for love first and for equality among humans before God. Moreover, the kingdom of the Father does not expand throughout the globe but in the heart of man. Also, the disciples look at each other with astonishment when they hear that the poor in the Spirit inherit the earth with their spirits, and that the kingdom of heaven is within them. Jesus has provided them with the necessary means to reach happiness, and His request to love their enemies as themselves and to bless those who curse them no longer surprises them. The river of love overflowing from His heart carries them with Him. In his presence, everything became accessible. The teacher placed the life of the inner Soul above all external exercises, the internal over the external, and the kingdom of heaven over the kingdoms of Earth. In his answer to Nicodemus, the chief of the Jews, said, "... if a man is not born from above, he cannot see the kingdom of God." Then He said to him, "If a man is not born of water and Spirit, he cannot enter the kingdom of God. He who is born of the flesh is flesh, and he who is born of the Spirit is spirit. Do not be surprised that I told you, you should be born "from above". The wind blows wherever it wants and you can hear its sound, but you do not know where it comes from nor where it goes, so is everyone born from the Spirit."

In Islam, there is a category that says that religious texts have two meanings: one is visible and understood by people through language, and through knowledge of speech, and the second is hidden, which is only perceived by those whom God has assigned this knowledge. Therefore, we find many interpretations that many disagree about, which that generated different Islamic groups. The editing of a text is not by its removal from its geographical and historical context, in which it originated, but through tracking its movement and what was added to it from accumulations or lack thereof. The moment the secondary text repeats what the original text has said, it has deviated from the authenticity of this text and given it a new interpretation. The missing link is that we have stopped at what has been said in the past and have not worked at knowing what could be said about it in our time. The receptive variables prevent the text from being spoken on its own, because it needs contemporary reading. The statements of the interpretations impose themselves and limit the spaces of the original text, which impedes the process of direct reception between the reader and him.

I concluded that no one can be where I am. In addition, the road I'm on, no one can take it. The sciences that I learned and the culture that I acquired, by spirit, mind, and wisdom, no one can obtain and no one can live them as I do. The person who I am, no one can be, and the mind that I possess, no one can borrow from me, nor can I impart it to anyone. My happiness is seeing dreams come true, and the atmosphere is filled with melancholy and joy, where the soul sees itself in the mirror of reality and rests assured. I go out of myself to see it from a distance, and I see it as a glow of light, a restless movement, and an indescribable source of happiness. My heart yearns for those moments when the causes are associated with their results, so I wipe my eyes, the tears of joy, from meeting the truth. This vast universe was created for me and I for it, so that my soul swims in the signs of the gods and learn. Every morning, I thank God who saved me, restored my conscious awareness, and a steady memory and a satisfied smile. The joy of God has cheered me, seized my dreams and visions, dwelt in my greatest soul, and wiped my sorrow forever. He took my parents and siblings, one after the other, and left me alone holding His hand. I am the man who touched the thorns of the earth with his bare feet and walked barefoot, treading on dirt, stones, and wet grass. I was looking at things around me, seeing them with the eye of the mind and the eye of the heart, and drowsed behind the horizon. There was my homeland, and from there I came to my body, every morning, on the wings of pink dreams. Since my childhood, I have spoken to myself in its silence, and kept up with it in the journey of existence. Who am I, I wonder, to hear the voices of meanings and see their charming beauty, other than that spirit that wore my body, and was enlightened by the lights of wisdom! I had no desire for life, except for seeing the joy on the children's faces, the ability to wipe the sadness from the faces of the old and the widows, and infuse love into souls. For this great goal, I sought, from a very early age, to enter the sanctuary of silence, and to gain knowledge of the intrinsic, after considering their phenomena. I found that science is necessary to decipher the mysteries of assets, to know how the event took place, without being able to figure out why it was. Dreams helped me reconcile with my younger self because I knew it for what it was, and I felt very ashamed for leaving it ignorant. My battle began by looking for the truth of things, where my weapon was limited to good and pure intentions. I sailed away from my home, my parents, and my family, and the waves were strong, bringing my boat up and down. I was terrified, with the fear of crashing, before reaching the shore of safety. In my practical life, I could not find a beach I could trust to find my aim, so the farther my boat anchored, the more I searched for a peaceful place in which my soul could rest. There is nothing that I can trust without finding the interest of others in it, as if there is no love for the sake of love, no art for the sake of art, and no gratuitous giving! The world has become a small village ruled by capitalism, greed, consumerism, and the tyranny of the weak. Life is indeed weariness and comfort, pursuit and reward, but weariness is lost in the presence of fraud, and the pursuit does not lead to a result in the presence of thieves, and nothing lasts if there is an endless change. Many times, I had experiences that I considered spiritual, and they all failed, or not as I desired. I trusted in divine providence as if it were my faithful servant. The result was not so, because dealing with others requires knowledge, readiness, diplomacy, good manners, and good timing. There is no dispensing of science in any of the fields, nor dispensing with the psychological and spiritual balance, that can only be achieved through satisfaction of what we have reached in terms of awareness, acquisition, and conviction in esoteric matters. We cannot deny the existence of esoteric thinking to carry out an exoteric work, and say that behind every exoteric there is the esoteric, is true. A grain of wheat grows for months under the ground to sprout a spike, carrying wheat. In autumn, a tree is stripped of its leaves, and it seems to us that its branches are devoid of life; but when spring comes, life sprouts in its roots, and the green leaves and flowers grow again.

Thus, when a person is created, his subconscious mind is created first, which is connected to the universal mind, then the conscious mind (the objective mind and the exoteric mind). It is as if the human mind lives in a three-floor villa: the objective mind lives on the highest floor, the exoteric mind lives on the middle floor, and the subconscious mind lives on the lowest floor. The subconscious mind communicates with the universal mind and acquires wisdom and ability. Whereas, the exoteric mind connects the objective mind with the esoteric mind in some way. We can imagine the exoteric mind as a repository of all our memories, as we do not forget anything. Moreover, our exoteric mind contains a large prison of all our desires, yearnings, feelings, and tendencies that we tried to keep away, and our consciousness is the jailer or the prison warden! The prisoners who are subject to our exoteric mind are the ones responsible for all our physical and psychological diseases. If we suffer from a neurological disorder, persistent anxiety, breakdown, hysterical symptoms, irritable anger, inability to concentrate, insomnia, lack of social orientation, persistent doubt, chronic hesitancy, obsessive thoughts, compulsive action, heart palpitations, constipation or anorexia, or any other pain for reasons or without physical reasons, then there is a great chance that one prisoner of our exoteric mind is the main reason! The human being is born a blank slate, on which his conscious mind (objective and exoteric) writes on all that he has acquired from parenting and life experiences, which his subconscious mind receives and regulates and assists him in choosing the behaviors that suit his goals, provided they are clear. The odd thing is that it works best in two situations: when a person thinks a lot about something and when he does not think at all. The subconscious mind is the depository of our memories, information, and habits, working day and night, even in our dreams.

The dreams that occur between waking and light sleep are, in general, predictive dreams, because the subconscious is in harmony with the memory of the universe, where it envelops its creative ideas and inner peace. The subconscious mind is the unconscious of the human being, and it is responsible for thoughts and dreams, for a person's mood, for determining true personality traits, and it is obedient to the human being, which can be directed by repetition. The collective unconscious is the reservoir of unconscious aspects that humanity shares in its infusion, which goes back to myths, religions, and superstitions. Can we consider the subconscious the fountain of knowledge from which we draw our vision, philosophy, and revelation? This question will not appeal to philosophers and may interest psychologists such as Carl Jung and Roberto Assagioli. Here is the great challenge, because there is no knowledge outside the mind. How can we achieve certain knowledge by means not dependent on reason, such as intuition, for example? Intuition is the ability to understand something by primitiveness or instinct, without the need for the mind's analysis. Instinct is the inclination towards an inner feeling, even if it is contradictory to what we have learned. There is a feeling that suddenly appears in our consciousness so clear that we can decide about it, without knowing why it happened. Intuition is the process that occurs in the mind without analysis, extending the bridges between the conscious and the unconscious, and between instinct and the mind. We need both mind and instinct to make the best personal, familial, and professional decisions. What is unfortunate is that many of us, when faced with success using less of our mental means, are not psychologically comfortable using our instincts to guide us. They do not trust some of the encrypted messages that come from their instincts, thus reducing their ability to use them when they need them. The discomfort we feel when we trust our instincts is due to a culture of pre-judgment. Therefore, we must trust fully what we feel when our thinking stops, because that means that we are in communication with our inner voice, which is the voice of God, or the voice of truth. When we trust our instinct, then we have moved from the world of senses to a world of heartfelt feelings that reflect the reality of what we are feeling in the direction of our experiences. Therefore, our sensory knowledge is a conscious, mental, incomplete knowledge, and it needs unconscious knowledge, which we acquire by premonition or by the sixth sense, i.e., intuition. When we pre-feel meeting someone, just moments before meeting them, or know who will talk to us when we hear the phone ringing, then our sixth sense is active. This is due to the state of internal peace we live in, or the lack of intellectual distortion of our psychological state. Therefore, intellectual emptiness, or the state of conscious unconsciousness, is the appropriate condition for inner peace and thus for intuitive work. The subconscious world is the world of the unconscious; we enter it every day, during our sleep and dreams. Between wake and sleep, the revelations are deep and spiritually meaningful. The development of the third eye and the third ear is only evidence of the development of the esoteric consciousness.

The human being is considered a rational animal because he uses his conscious mind to restrain his passions, to control them, and to use logic, deduction, and reason to reach the results that help him make his decisions. However, sometimes, the answers to his questions come to him, without an effort from him, from his subconscious unconscious mind, in the form of revelation and inspiration, to his conscious mind. When deciding on critical matters, we return to what the heart tells us, even though it is silent as the silence of the Sphinx. What can it say, and where did it get it? The heart, metaphorically, unconsciously, or subconsciously, does not act on its own, but obeys the conscious mind in what it asks. However, when information is stored in it, there is no need to remind it of it, because it takes the initiative on its own, and helps the person succeed in their mission. Thus, we see the professional athlete relax, to allow his subconscious mind, perform his task. On the other hand, we see the thief or the criminal doing his work confidently, because his subconscious mind is incapable of making moral judgments. The subconscious mind is an anonymous character that does not distinguish wrong from right, and this responsibility falls on the conscious mind alone. All the person's voluntary actions are directly subject to the conscious mind, while his involuntary actions are subject to the subconscious, as are all other beings, who have no will, but are subject to their instincts, and act instinctively. The subconscious mind remains idle because it has no goals to achieve if it does not receive instructions from the conscious mind. Hence, the importance of the conscious mind's task of informing the subconscious mind what it wants, and then the profound belief that it will get what it wants. Here, fear, anxiety, and confusion must be expelled from the conscious mind, because those who have fears are likely to materialize. You must know how to communicate with your subconscious mind because it will solve your problems, inspire you with new ideas, you will know how to use intuition successfully, you will feel more relaxed and confident, and you will be able to achieve your dreams. When you are faced with a difficult problem, you will receive guidance somewhere from within. You must learn how to relax and meditate in a quiet place and wait for the right answers. Strangely enough, there is no need to have experience to program your subconscious mind because it responds to facts and to what you imagine. All you must do is ask for what you want and seek to find what you want. If this is accompanied by a belief that everything can be achieved, you will achieve what you want. You can get everything you imagine if you believe in the possibility of its achievement: a new car, a bigger house, a better job, or a happier family life. All of this is possible if you believe in it.

Your subconscious mind will automatically achieve whatever you want, according to its programming, whether it's reality or fiction. What is the difference between the subconscious and our perception of God, if all that we ask or imagine, we can get? Is this not the simple man's belief in the existence of a supreme being, the Creator of the heavens and the earth and everything in between, that helps him to overcome obstacles and achieve his wishes? I say yes and no! There is a need for the believer to pass through the conscious mind so that he can choose exactly what he wants, because the responsibility falls on him. There is no comparison between God, the supreme being, and the subconscious mind, which performs what the conscious mind demands, even if it is evil.

***

12. Consumptive Materialism

Our present era is characterized by crazy developments, such as the means of communication, scientific inventions, the avidity of societies to consume everything new, excess freedoms and low morals, and the rich getting richer and the poor getting poorer. This materialism sees the primacy of material over man and all his activities, and gives reason and morality a second place over the material. According to historical materialism, man is the result of a kinetic material process that assumes the precedence of matter over thought. Human life requires food, drink, housing, and clothing, and these things are not readily found in nature; he must produce and market them. Thus, social relations arise, and the person's consciousness, outlooks, and aspirations are formed. As such, it constitutes the ultimate production that determines the lifestyle of people, their consciousness, their intellect, and their entire spiritual and social life. Thus, the essence of life remains material, otherwise, it is accidental transformations, and the center of the universe in the material world. The main purpose of human beings has become the material goods that life provides. This material heresy cannot speak of the non-material aspects such as morals, aesthetics, and spirituality. It is not content with explaining some aspects of reality, but insists on explaining all aspects of life, including the human being. It finds it easier to talk about the material without talking about the abstract, the mind, imagination, and emotions, which are not directly related to the body. Man becomes part of the whole, without an identity or a will independent of this material entity. Infusing with nature is the loss of consciousness, identity, boundaries, and in it the victory of the subject over the self, and this threatens the humanity of mankind, which is the essence of all heresies hostile to God and man. The truth calls for stability and universality, and a world that transcends our material world. It is not possible to trust closed worlds, nor in rigid causation, because whenever a person discovers and controls something, a thousand new things appear to him that he does not know and cannot control. Moreover, the discovery of the black hole showed that the laws of nature and biology are destroyed, along with time and space, and light, the fixed element in nature, is consumed. The assumption that the world was created by accident has no scientific certainty. Some believe in the spiritual unity of existence and the subsequent emanations of God in beings. God becomes nature, the absolute spirit, or the spirit of history. Also, some believe in the physical unity of existence, and any spiritual or idealistic language is dispensed, so that the laws of nature prevail. In both, there is unity, not duality, which unites man with nature and eliminates all dualities in a final secular absolute, which turns the world into a relativistic physical reality. Here, material facts are separate from values, and appear to be science that is separate from morality, and from human, religious, emotional, and moral ends, and the changing material realities become the only acceptable cognitive reference. This materialistic monistic vision, by denying any immutability, ends up denying the existence of reality and essence, and even of human nature itself. It is the world of comprehensive secularism and rationalization in the material context. The human being contains within him elements that transcend the laws of movement and the natural order, which constitute the essence of man.

***

13. The Problematic of the Natural and the Human

The human is a being that greatly exceeds our current perceptions. The body is the temple of its creator, which contains several sensitive centers, through which life's energy emerges. There are seven energy centers (chakras) that work like windows, allowing the body to breathe spiritually. The closer a person is to the harmony of energy within him, the greater the sense of balance and understanding of the process of the transformation of sensations into feelings, into thoughts, and experiences in the present. How can we integrate man with material nature when he is completely different from it and other beings? Natural science deals with the aspects of physical reality in all its details. The method of study is direct observation and repeated and diverse experimentation, until we reach a generalization about the existence of fixed relationships between phenomena. Whereas, in the study of the human personality, we find an unspecified number of elements, impossible to disintegrate. Moreover, when the part is separated from the whole, the whole vibrates and changes completely, and the part loses its meaning. The natural phenomenon is a repetitive unit of causes and effects, and generalizes judgment on it in the past, present, and future. However, the human phenomenon is always an isolated case, and we cannot find two similar situations. The natural phenomenon is subject to objective laws that move it from the outside, while the human phenomenon has a free will and consciousness that determines behavior, a memory that makes a person connect the past to the present, a conscience that makes him behave differently, and a feeling that gives a new color to the lived reality. In natural phenomena, there is an organic association between the exterior and the interior, governed by very precise laws. As for human phenomena, its exterior is different from its interior, due to dreams, symbols, and awareness, so that science has not been able to observe the inner experience of man and explain his pent-up emotions and his possible or impossible dreams. If the natural phenomenon is devoid of space and time, without awareness, memory, or will, then the human phenomenon is formed by the act of culture, which varies from one environment to another. Also, the natural phenomenon is not influenced by the experiments conducted on it because it is subject to the natural program, unlike the human phenomenon, which is affected by the experiments conducted on it. After all, it is placed under the microscope, and individuals change their behavior, consciously or unconsciously, since they are under observation. Finally, whoever studies the natural phenomenon is not affected by it, neither from near nor from afar, but is stripped of his ambitions and interests, and deals with them objectively. As for the human phenomenon, it is impossible for the researcher not to respond to his emotions and prejudices through his moral values and aesthetic systems, or to strip himself of his passions, interests, and values. It has become clear to us how difficult it is to integrate the human being into material nature because they differ in essence. To respect his freedom and his will, we must look at his basic formation and what suits him so that the reservoirs of his soul can be opened up, to achieve self-realization as he desires. The responsibility of the researcher is to prepare the natural environment for human growth in his environment so that it is clean and sound of disabilities and able to secure internal peace in the human being, so that he takes the right path for himself and his surroundings. Here emerge the noble goals of our presence on earth and our responsibility to achieve those universal humanitarian goals.

***

14. Man of this Age

A person of this age is no longer like a person of the rest of the ages, because he has walked on the path of scientific discoveries and evoked an unimaginable past and a future close to flying saucers. Erich von Daniken spoke of runways for airports that creatures from other planets land on with their vehicles. With the development of the means of communication, we are now close to data information, in which rumor is mixed with information and is seldom documented.

A little over fifty years ago, the quantum physicist revolutionized the world of the atom, returning everything to vibrations or frequencies, and we all live in a comprehensive electromagnetic field. However, man has remained unable to determine the purpose of life; as such, people followed different beliefs. Some adopted religious beliefs, claiming that there is a creator of this universe, paradise, and bliss.

Some denied these beliefs and believed in human materialism, and that his end is annihilation. Finally, some believe in reincarnation and the return of the human after death into other living beings. What is unfortunate is that many well-known personalities committed suicide, even though they knew a life of well-being and success in their artistic careers. The price of psychological balance and acceptance of life as it is, requires beautiful patience and addressing the problems of understanding carefully and choosing the point from which things are viewed, and to approach things realistically and steadily.

The human being is born a blank slate, where his family and community inscribe many legacies, until he develops an inner sense of things, so that the perceptions of awareness and understanding expand, he gets rid of his selfishness, and he works to build a better society. If we cannot identify something in detail, nor know why it occurred, then we should look for ways to find out how it happened. Life needs to be looked at by the eyes of reason, the heart, and wisdom so that there can be salvation for human society. It is possible to help someone who was born with an illness, whether physical or psychological. However, it is difficult to help a person who lives in an environment that nurtures a certain type of confinement, believes in the occult, and practices magic in all its forms. On the other hand, a person raised with a specific behavior does not accept dialogue, or understand the course of events in a different way, and finds it impossible to change paths. If people have imprinted and drank, involuntarily, on a certain number of whims that are difficult to abandon, such as smoking, alcoholism, drugs, and gambling, then how can they abandon their extremist behaviors without them acquiring knowledge, wisdom, foresight in taking positions, and seeking to maintain the middle path in everything? What stopped me was abandoning the idea of changing others, based on the distance that separates us from one another, from the cultural considerations and the different lifestyles that divide us, and replacing that with changing my understanding to a more realistic and clearer understanding of the differences between us. As for what I see as a halo around others, that they do not see, they need to believe in its existence to develop knowledge. Spirituality and faith go hand in hand because the system of the human spirit consists of a hidden presence to express our spirituality. There are sensitive centers (chakras) to monitor the vitality of the body, pleasures, will, love, relationships, wisdom, perception, which are considered mental and psychological.

***

15. How Beliefs are Formed

In their private and community life, human beings learn a useful lesson, from noble insects, like ants, bees and beetles, who work hard and steadfastly to collect their food, without complaint or boredom, as if they came to carry out a mission embedded in their genes, withing a total system for the sake of the unity of this universe. The ant Kingdom is characterized by cooperation among its members to transport supplies, defend the weak, and protect the group. Whereas, the bee Kingdom is characterized by its architectural system, guardianship, knowledge of the sources of their industry, communication between each other, and the harvesting of honey, which is beneficial to human health. However, the beetle kingdom is distinguished by the rules of public health, by taking its waste out of its burrow and burying it away from it. As for the kingdom of motherhood, it is present in all animals and birds that seek to teach their young how to search for their food and hide when there is an external danger. This blind trust, and this giving in to the matters of life, in all beings, has led the monotheistic religions to direct the attention of their followers to fact that there is a God who cares for them, just as He cares also about the flowers in the fields, and He's the one who sustains them if they believe in Him and obey his commandments. Some religious groups, especially Muslims, have come to believe in "fate and destiny", whether good or evil. God, here, in the three monotheistic religions, is a Person, unlike any other person, who conceals His appearance, who is the Creator of the heavens, the earth, and what is in between, and intervenes in human matters when necessary. Religious doctrines were formed that differed among themselves over the interpretation of the religious text, and they obtained followers over the length and width of the land. I am not here to accept or reject what others believe, but I strongly support the human right to freedom of belief, as long as no one on earth can give them security, reassurance, and a convincing answer to their questions about life and death. We have seen how many successful people in their careers و who have not found a convincing answer to their questions and have chosen to commit suicide. The belief in giving up the responsibilities of life to those who we think are better than us is an escape from responsibility and throwing it on others. This is not what the ant or the bee teaches us, if we are worthy of a life of solidarity with the members of our society. The Earth is now spherical and not infinitely flat. The superstitious view of religion cannot be reconciled with what science has learned about the shape of the earth, its resources, its population, the ways to ensure the needs of its inhabitants, and the fight against poverty, hunger, and unemployment. Apart from religious beliefs, there are complex life matters that everyone must unite to overcome through science and experience. There is no salvation for the individual alone; there is either salvation for us all or no salvation for anyone. The story of the ancients, and sitting under the tree and meditating, helped many to understand themselves, and developed beliefs towards the common good, but it no longer meets the purpose of development that we need today, as a group of people living in a small village called Earth. We live in an age that is more than a thousand years after the passage of the ancients, and we have developed with science, reason, and understanding to reveal the hidden secrets of our lost humanity. Our old strains will disappear because we need someone to enter us into the "Age of Light, Love and Solidarity", not to occupy us with discrimination, hatred, and futile wars.

16. Leap of Faith

According to Jewish teachings, a Jew is one whose mother is Jewish and has converted to Judaism in turn. Some rabbis say that a Jew does not have to follow Jewish law or traditions to be considered Jewish. Moreover, a person is considered Jewish, even if he has no faith in God at all. Whereas other rabbis clarify that unless a person follows the teachings of the Torah and accepts the thirteen basic principles of faith of Maimonides, then he is not considered a Jew. Today, many believe that a Jew is a descendant of Abraham, Isaac, and Jacob, regardless of the original tribe to which they already belong.

Faith in Christianity: The Boy with a Demon,

…19 Afterward, the disciples came to Jesus privately and asked, "Why couldn't we drive it out?" 20"Because you have so little faith," He answered. "For truly I tell you, if you have faith the size of a mustard seed, you can say to this mountain. 'Move from here to there,' and it will move. Nothing will be impossible for you." … (Matthew 20:17)

Jesus Heals the Man Born Blind

…6 When Jesus had said this, He spat on the ground, made some mud, and applied it to the man's eyes. 7 Then He told him, "Go, wash in the pool of Siloam" (which means Sent). Therefore, the man went and washed, and came back seeing. (John 9 6).

Faith in Islam is known as a safe source that secures faith, it is a believer, and it is from security, that is, against fear. Faith takes place if it is settled in the heart with absolute belief and submission to Allah. In the Prophet's Hadith, when Jibril (Gabriel) came and the Prophet Mohammed asked him about faith, Islam, and charity, and that is when "he said: tell me about faith. "He said: 'Belief is your belief in Allah, His angels, His books, His messengers, Judgement Day, and all of Destiny; His good and bad. "He said: I accept.' These are the six pillars of Islam.

This is faith according to the three monotheistic religions, which give importance to faith in their beliefs so that the believer receives salvation. The problem is that religions came to divide people from each other and not to unite them into one human family, nor to accept diversity.

As for what psychology says, a firm belief is the necessary basis for the work of the subconscious mind, and to achieve what the conscious mind demands and imagines. However, the problem is that the human being hides since childhood the ideas and feelings that are difficult to declare to those around them. This is known as suppression, which is a set of forces that prevent pent-up feelings from reaching the conscious mind, so it is collected and stored in the subconscious mind. It could be feelings of aggression, feelings of hatred toward certain people, feelings of shame or fear, and their suppression may lead to problems that are difficult to cure in the future, such as depression, anxiety, or stress. Moreover, the subconscious mind is blind and indifferent to morality, which means that it executes all that is required of it. To avoid these problems, it is necessary to select the correct and useful information given to the subconscious mind.

From here, I had my path in the search for internal peace and remaining a friend with religion and science as long as they do not order what is contrary to the rights of the individual and the community, and all that would not evolve towards a single and comprehensive humanity. Some things are difficult to understand right away, and a decision must be made with patience. How is it possible to believe everything that religion says about the unseen, and how can one reach a state of absolute faith, without intimidation or fear from any party?

There are things in life that cannot be changed, such as birth, death, God, and the universe, although our view of them is the one that changes according to our cultural and religious level and according to our aesthetic view of existence. Culture increases our viewpoints and allows us to compare with other sensual, psychological, mental, and spiritual perceptions so that we can examine several facts and correct our vision. If we look at primitive tribes in a part of the world, we see that they left graphics and statues like those left by other tribes located in a place distant from them, without any contact between them. This proves, according to Carl Jung, that there is a connection between them through the collective unconscious, which is the storehouse of human ethnic experience. Culture is everything ideal, what the elite meet, and everything that is closely related to the arts in general. Whereas religion is about the set of ideas and beliefs that explain the purpose of life and the universe, related to that beyond nature, divinity, and morality, and what is related to the practices and institutions associated with those beliefs that extend beyond the family, government, and politics. Religion helps people deal with the important human life problems.

The monotheistic religions have unanimously agreed on many things among themselves, and each religion has approved and added more to what preceded it. The religious text in general has been subject to changes over time and has several projections that need interpretation. Reading the religious text from a historical or rational point of view does not fulfill the desired purpose; rather, it is a departure from the realization of the goal of the existence of religion in societies, especially primitive ones, that is, the involvement of the unseen to protect from the unknown through revelation!

Religion was built on the unseen, secrets, interpretations, behaviors, and rituals practiced by its followers. In every religion, there is an intolerant fundamentalism that has taken its understanding of the religious text to justify what it seeks by violence, and to deliver salvation to humanity or to the environment to which it belongs. Also, some reformers coexist with other religions depending on the circumstances. Doctrine is cruel and necessary at the same time. It cannot not be, nor can it be other than what it is, since there are phenomena of being and life. That is, the supreme being is, and it is useless to imagine another being; however, we must confess to Him that He is the cause of life.

There is a universal system that permeates everything, and there is a life that derives its unity from that system. A believer needs a "Leap of Faith" into the common space between religions in which he sees the unity of the whole in the part and the unity of the part in the whole. However, this may happen to a small, conscious group, but fanatic fundamentalists want to use violence to achieve their goals.

There is no doubt that all heavenly religions are inherently violent because of the exclusivity that encourages violence against those who are considered strangers to the religion. Moreover, if we go back in history, we find that **monotheistic religions have a legacy and a history of violence, and that history is a genocide**. Therefore, the task of the reformists was to stop the violence first and to come up with a new concept of interfaith coexistence, based on cooperation and mutual respect.

The idea of secularism, which is the separation of religion from the state, goes along with some principles of liberalism. What modernity required of secularism was a reaction against religious violence in the 16th and 17th centuries. It confirms that secularism was a means to live with religious differences that produced a lot of terror. Many religious practitioners have collectively emphasized the need for dialogue and cooperation among religions, an emphasis on universal values, and recognition of the diversity of religious practices among different cultures. The problem is that this awareness has not spread enough to encompass all circles, and it has not been given sufficient attention to educate young people and to continue raising them. Moreover, the multiplicity of schisms between the doctrines has led to the emergence of a group of fundamentalist fanatics.

However, secularism was not acceptable, one day, that is because some religious people view it as infidelity and atheism, and because some who claim secularism stand with dictatorships and wage a war against the religious. The solution may be to establish scientific research, develop individual potentialities, and involve them in joint developmental projects. Secularism, in general, is in the separation of religion from the state, education, and ethics, and human interest must be in this present life and not in the afterlife, and thus rejects the occult. Secularism is concerned with the rights, freedoms, and equality of all before the law.

Philosophy may not find a way to reconcile secularism with religion, because it adopts reason alone in realizing the truth, while art recognizes inspiration, which is a kind of revelation, in arriving at the truth through intuition. Therefore, the separation of religion from the state is not by denying occult facts, but by cooperating with religion in organizing society based on purely human grounds that depend on rationality, experiments, and systematic scientific research. Secularism seeks to improve human life in this world by practical, pragmatic, material means. Science is indeed the destiny of man, but he must believe in divine providence, on the other hand. As well as doing good in this world, it is reciprocated to the person who does it; however, goodness must be done for its own sake to make human life as happy as possible.

The world is moving towards unity, the unity of the conscience and the unity of the goal, indifferent to the hatred, intolerance, and fanaticism produced by some of the stray groups, and that human intelligence is more powerful than weapons, killing, and displacement. Perhaps it allows idiots to go on their way to reap what their hands had sown.

The "New Age" is the era of high values and dealing with the universal virtues for a just and comprehensive peace. That is what **I saw** a long time ago, and this is what I see now. Perhaps I do not dream, but I see with my own eyes everything that happens, and it may be difficult to conclude. Time has changed, wars may be to impose peace, darkness may be to reveal light, lies may be to reveal facts, and the march of return may be a new departure forward. Do not forget that darkness is the absence of light, and evil is the absence of good. Silence is the word of the wise, but even the commandments of the gods. We must know that the existent is the one that reflects the authenticity of existence with the values that he possesses, and in his earnest and persistent search to prove compatibility, harmony, and reconciliation between wisdom and law. The human being is the primary concern in everything that humanity aspires to in the depths of its journey towards perfection. The goal of existence is the salvation of the existent in unity, the depth of consciousness, and the peace of the soul. The human being, in his birth, is like any other being, in terms of the need for tenderness, constant care, and nourishment. All beings cease to evolve to follow their instincts, except for the human being, who needs to raise awareness within themselves, acquire science, and educate themselves to rise towards ideals and higher values, to be enlightened by them, and take responsibility in life to build a good, peaceful, and prosperous society. The biggest problem is that no matter how advanced a person is, they cannot pass their knowledge on to anyone.

Therefore, the evolution is a matter of rebuilding personality from one generation to another.

***

17. Discovering our Humanity

In closed societies, where ignorance and intolerance prevail, we find it difficult to get rid of old legacies, because, firstly, we are deprived of our freedom, and secondly, because we do not develop in mind and spirit. Rather, we are defeated by the constraints of our societies that deny us our fundamental rights. In this case, the human is but a talking animal, turning in vicious circles, concerned with meeting the demands of religion and its oppressive authority. However, in liberal societies, the human being is subject only to the rule of law, away from religious authority, which does not interfere with politics. The upbringing of the individual in such societies is based on the respect of the individual and the knowledge of their respective rights and duties, allowing them freedom in matters of religiosity. These societies evolve towards a universal humanity whose purpose is in the unity of the "human family"

as a whole. People are similar, but the existence of the individual is determined, in a better way, according to their companionship and the people that one decides to surround oneself with. Kind-hearted people are the best, with them you can learn about your inner experience and its transformations. However, you must first come to terms with a society of citizenship, where law, peace, freedom, justice, and democracy prevail. Nevertheless, there are various origins and strategies with which both the individual and collective memories can be activated to resist the authority of the ancients. This helps overcome the current frustrations due to the prevalence of double standards in dealing with human rights and the public silence over the violations of practices of well-known groups to undermine the authority of law and the state. We must define what the correct citizenship is, as well as agree on the country we want, whether it is a secular state or a civil one or a mosaic that is balanced among its different currents and sects, which unanimously agree not to contravene and to establish **"unity in diversity"**. We must respect all opinions and stop violating and suppressing the rights and freedoms of the citizens who demand dignity and social justice. There is a false awareness that must stop because it is based on intimidation and the exchange of freedom for factional preventive security. We must look for the positive aspects in reviving the heritage based on the noble values that were brought up by the generations that have achieved independence. This would be by cutting all contact with the outside world and renouncing all populist commitments aimed at erasing the original national identity. Those high aspirations that committed itself to a free and independent nation, have been absent from the arena of citizenship, and we need to restore it packed with its best memories, to lead generations again to a culture of accepting the other, pluralism and respecting the other's right to exist, love, beauty, and life. Enough marginal wars, in which we lost the flower of our youth; I do now know whether they were necessary or not. History will judge these wars; it will judge us, as well as those who contributed to igniting them. We must heal from these wounds and recover from what is going on around us. This may be done by involving the United Nations in the responsibility of maintaining our security, before neighboring countries invade parts of our land, dear to our hearts, and before displacing the rest of our people. If the nation remains in its present state, a battlefield between Zayd and Amr, between religions, between neighboring countries, and between powerful countries, its value as an unmatched human civilization will die, because it will give up the reason for its existence, being a refuge for peoples of different religion, race, customs and cultures, and a message of love that unites nations.

18. Free Steps

One day of my busy youth, a Visitor came to me in the night, knocking on my door steadily. His face was lost in the darkness, but his words were so confident that they established peace in my heart. He looked at me lengthily, and spoke to me words that encouraged me to listen to him. He told me that he would help me cross the river to the other bank, provided I prepare myself for this exceptional life experience. He extended his hand to shake my hand firmly, telling me that he would always be with me, and unleashing his steps, hiding under the shades of darkness.

I returned to my hermitage, enchanted by this meeting, which I had been waiting for years. Finally, it became certain to me that there is a path that leads the seeker of knowledge to discover his truth about himself and how to communicate with the creative forces in existence. I went to my garden asking the flowers how they bloom, and how the trees cover themselves with green leaves. Also, I knew that there is a replay of the supposed first creation process, during the Earth's rotation around itself and around the sun; circumstances allowed me to live in an area where the four seasons begin and end on time. I felt that there was some magic in nature, bringing back to life what appears to be dead, and that, as the sun rises every morning, new life comes to earth. However, darkness does not exist by itself; it is the absence of light, and death does not exist by itself, but it is the absence of life. Moreover, I found that there is a secret in nature that no one knows, which is the secret of life and death. We know how birth takes place, but we do not know how life enters the body, and why. Until now, there has been a dilemma that is difficult to solve, which is that there is no consensus between the assumptions, religious and scientific, about the origin of existence. The difference exists between the assumption of the existence of creatures with a Creator and a certain age, and the presence of beings that began with the universe, and their age is the age of time, including the human being! However, nature has created them with superior wisdom, so that they know how to seek to reap their strength, to be clean, to communicate with one another, or to defend the members of their race. These creatures instinctively work to the fullest, and we began to wonder how humans have suppressed their instinct by material gains and have become in need of serenity, meditation, and distancing from the noise of ideas. There is great benefit in communicating with the spirit center, which is an expanse of luminous observations, that helps us to see clearly and make better choices. The human being is indeed composed of the spirit, the soul, and the body, each with its potentialities and energies, which develop with knowledge and experience. We must not confuse them so that the individual acts with full awareness of his potential, and manages the helm of government. Perhaps I can say that there is a spirit that enters the formation of the soul and the body and makes them what they are. The spirit has a divine source, immaterial, and the soul shares the characteristics of the spirit and the body, and connects them, and the body is earthly with material components. For me, the soul is the personality that develops according to its events and earthly experiences, and rises and returns to complete the journey. The goal of life is to purify the human being from the pillars of matter and learn the lessons of life. If we assume that the Spirit is complete and unchanging, due to its divine source, then the soul or the human personality is the one that changes and acquires its spiritual qualities through experience.

Father Pierre Teilhard de Chardin says that a human being is a soul having an earthly experience, not a body having a spiritual experience. Life is a conscious experience, it is a conflict with our misperceptions, and a transition of knowledge, from the dark to the light. Evil is present, and it is at work in our lives, where violence, isolation, rejection of the other, tyranny, and wars appear, and it does not work when it does not find leniency from us and acceptance of it to enter our lives. Father Teilhard de Chardin was right when he considered the universe a "living host"; also, he declared at a conference in Paris in 1931: "The observers of the future must wait for the greatest event, which is the sudden emergence of the collective conscience of humanity and human action."

He also wrote about the discovery of the physical universe, from the fundamental particles to the evolution of life and human beings, that is, the mental field, and finally, to develop towards the omega point in the future, which "pulls" all creation towards it. One means of development is the culture, which is accomplished using education and upbringing. However, evolution has become an increasingly optional process, since social problems of isolation and marginalization discourage it, as evolution requires the unification of consciousness. An individual's development can't take place through voluntary collective solidarity. This may be done through a voluntary psychological unity of humanity. Evolution is the ascent towards consciousness, towards the Omega point, when intentions and purposes are recognized. Divine love was a source of polarization for the prophets and apostles, who were at the height of their enlightenment, and in whom divine mercy was placed. We can meditate for ourselves when consciousness becomes an energy of love, living in a whirlpool, and the closer we are to its center, the more its foundations will be built. Perhaps the one who has reached a state of enlightenment can amaze humankind with the universal energy of love that he has acquired. However, humanity will collapse and the energy will be concentrated in one point, automatically rising to the rank of light and love. This may happen at the end of history, and until then, humanity needs to take firm steps towards getting rid of its negatives and gaining the positives. The development of societies begins with the evolution of the individual in an environment of freedom and democracy. This seems elusive to societies that are closed to themselves, intolerant of their culture, and ignorant. Tribes that live in the Amazon jungle or the Australian forests, and whose land has never been set foot on by a human being, first need to open to civilization by acquiring science, educating society, and then cultivating the cultures of developed countries. Moreover, people who live on raising livestock and fishing, or only on agriculture, must enter the world of industry and communications to market their products. The openness of people to one another will, of course, help to break the psychological barriers caused by seclusion. However, the gallery of politics and regulations can distort the clarity of this familiarity, by creating differences and side wars, that leave no room for peace and security. So, man remains concerned about his fate and the fate of his family, and remains on the move, from one country to another, seeking peace and comfort. Every human being has a leeway to live in. He must organize his life in a way that guarantees his psychological balance, the possibility of achieving his spiritual and practical aspirations, his well-being, and happiness throughout his life. How one reaches this stage is one of the most important goals that every sane person aspires to. However, societies differ according to their cultural heritage, their geographical location, and the means of modernization. Also, the human being, through their strengths, must overcome obstacles and perform miracles to pave the way that leads them to what they seek.

It was written at the entrance to the Temple of Apollo (Delphi): "Know thyself and you will know God and the universe". This means finding your true personality among the rubble of what you have inherited from your family and what you have acquired in life. It is a revealing experience that allows you to become self-sufficient and to do what benefits you in your life.

In my career, I have felt the Visitor's presence as an inner presence of light.

My story may be the best I can address because it is my personal experience, and what I have already experienced. Ever since I was young, I have been listening intently to everything that is happening around me and within me, from events, however simple. Which led me to awaken and pay attention to the hidden messages that it might carry for me. I used to record in my notebooks a timeline of my life, as children do in their prime. I wrote down all the important goals, the short-term and the long-term, that I had to achieve, to be reassured, satisfied, and happy, which formed my personality and influenced my formation. When life confronted me with its difficulties and problems, it drastically changed my way of thinking. This is what I consider a new experience in my life that helped me be who I am. Isolating myself and writing these diaries contributed in identifying past events and lessons learned, and looking for a way to accommodate them. I was not influenced by the ideas and attitudes of others, so that I would have a free space for creative and innovative behavior. I wondered a lot about what other people believed, and rejected everything that seemed superficial and meaningless, and I did not accept any preconceived convictions prevalent in my society. My intuition may have helped me to make the right decision, to avoid the fallacies that would inevitably lead to the destruction of my creative freedom and thus my personality. Therefore, I relied on myself for everything I searched for and everything I wanted to learn. I had blind faith in myself, even obstinate, and I relied on it. I had a strong belief in my ability, and the opinions of others did not appeal to me unless they were identical to what I felt. This is what prompted me to develop my sense of self and my ability to overcome difficulties and be patient in my belief that the right things must come on time. I was confident in my decisions, which were often wrong, and I thought that it was my mistakes that developed me, taught me, and led me to know myself. That sense of responsibility invited me, while I was still in school, to start teaching in private schools and earn my money, which secured me relative economic independence. It also helped me decide to get married six months before I got my postgraduate diploma in architecture. I had great faith in myself and absolute trust in the Divine Providence, because my intentions were sound and selfless, even altruistic. Moreover, I did not ignore the small details in life, but rather I gave them my attention, and I left nothing to the waves of "fate and destiny". However, life is not a straight line, but a meandering path that has kept me out of the way. This is what prompted me to develop my behavior by cutting off all harmful habits. In truth, there were no bad habits as much as they were an escape for me not to think about my life, taking up my time, and preventing me from benefiting from my full energy. In return, I was living an organized life that helped me clear my mind from my preoccupations, and made it possible to speed up my self-knowledge. Due to my distance from my family, I was able to take the necessary steps to save time every week, to research and study spiritual issues.

However, my circumstances were not conducive to evolution in many cases, so I sought to overcome them by isolating myself completely from my surroundings. I was giving myself some time to get rid of meeting others and watching the news, to pursue intellectual and artistic activities. It is true that the time allotted for walking, extended to thinking and meditating. There were a few subjects that distracted my thoughts and kept me from planning for my future. I felt free in my isolation and self-confident without fear or the need for anything. I renewed my activity and conversed with myself, in an atmosphere of peace, and being alone was not as bad as it freed me from my problems. That period helped me to meditate deeply in a comfortable musical atmosphere and to develop my faculty of reading. However, consulting with others, at times, was useful, but it was causing me to lose the faculty of Creativity.

At the beginning of my working life, I was a little lost, because I lacked the experience and still did not know yet my talents. I had great ambitions, such as going to military school, being a math teacher, working to protect and renovate heritage buildings, or being a university professor at the Institute of Fine Arts. However, they all failed in part for several reasons: for familial reasons, for personal reasons, and due to Lebanon's situation during the civil war in 1975, which lasted 15 years, until 1990. Yet, when I decided to study architecture, I gave myself all the confidence to succeed in my profession. However, the profession of architecture is complex and has multiple applications, including advisory, administrative, and technical. After bitter experiences in Riyadh and moving between contracting and consulting offices, I found myself managing the building workshops, especially the architectural section. Thus, I took turns in implementing major construction projects and gained extensive experience, which enabled me to successfully pursue my career in this field, whether in Riyadh, Dubai, or Cairo. It was difficult for me to set a goal and maintain it, due to the many pitfalls I encountered. Perhaps it was my search for something I love that saved me from the clutches of consumerism, traders, and capitalists, even though my life was at their service. What I think is that these are the ones who move the wheel of the economy, wherever it is, whether we like it or not, and we cannot do without them. My only interest was to work in the artistic field, with a living conscience, without error, and theft. It was important for me for my work to be well received by my superiors, and to be compensated for my efforts, but it did not happen as I wanted. I was chasing bonuses, and the bonuses were running from in front of me, with what happened from collisions with the employers, who I saw very much alike, in terms of a lack of fair appreciation of the employee, or terms of encouragement. However, what encouraged me to stay was the type of artwork that I contributed to creating and implementing, which gave me unparalleled psychological comfort. I was satisfied with my work because it did not lack any technical creativity and because I created an atmosphere of cooperation between those who were working under my direct supervision. I have established technical offices to prepare for the implementation of construction and interior decoration works, in each of Dubai (13 engineers, architects and draftsman) and in Cairo (35 engineers and 20 architects), where we were able to participate in the implementation of one of the largest projects in the Middle East. My belief in my work and my vision of the aesthetics in it helped me accept any emotional or financial pressures, especially since I was the head of a family. My goal was to secure the necessary expenses for education, medicine, housing, food, and all that they needed to be satisfied. What I think is that I found a family worthy of my efforts and sacrifices for them, because my children were among the best in their classes, and of high morals. I found the best path in my life, which led me, in the end, to the pursuit of life for a high and noble goal. I did not have a particular goal at first, but I found my passion in my work and succeeded in completing it perfectly. Every morning, I felt something urging me to get out of bed, even if I was sleepy, because something beautiful was awaiting me. Therefore, after exhausting all attempts to stay, I held on to my job until the last working day. the search was always about a work that had a touch of art, a bit of respect, and a sense of reassurance. This is what helped me develop my abilities through experience.

***

19. Transcendental Consciousness

Searching for oneself is one of the hardest things one can do. I do not forget that the first book I printed in Arabic was under the main title: "Searching for the Self in the secrets of the collective unconsciousness", with the subtitle: "A life path in the journeys of a Disciple". I used to and still believe that the collective unconscious is the vast lake, to which human thoughts and experiences flow since the beginning of existence. We have only to pick up from it the masterpieces of our arts and philosophies. However, the search for the self is not done with the partnership of anyone, because it is the human being who knows what he wants and how to reach it. Being open towards others and listening to the inner voice helps us not to lose advice from those who are qualified, especially when the doors close before us and we are faced with obstacles. I was, in that case, looking for someone to trust because of his self-confidence and ability to help. He was the one who made me feel that it was important to me and that I had to search for a solution, and he would do his best to help me. Perhaps what I had hoped for, in the early years of my pampered professional experience, was for the other to adopt a stance for me and pledge to me, but that would not have happened. I have learned a lot from my mistakes, from my failures, and from the repulse of those who were close to me, because they did not suffer what I suffered. Searching for a trustworthy person was one of the most important things that I encountered in my life, especially when I was witnessing the states of telepathy, anticipation, and intuition. It was the other's concern to advise me to search for money and to live luxuriously, which is something that he did not want for himself, nor could he have done. When I was applying for a scholarship outside of Lebanon, I came across Elias (and I do not know whether there are coincidences in life), a person in whom I found all the understanding of my situation, who gave me advice and a helping hand to start my life again, following my materialistic and spiritual ambitions.

I do not deny what happened to me in Riyadh, in the first years of my career outside Lebanon, from moving between different companies and jobs, to attain what suited me, because I was not happy. Of course, changing the company was an excuse for me because my awareness of my personal qualities was incomplete. Thanks to my interest in what I love to do, it helped me find the parts of myself that I tried to collect over time. I was in dire need of money, especially when I bought an apartment in the mountains and had to pay for it. How nervous I was in those days, with a series of professional pressures on me, and I sought help from my daily agenda, writing in it everything I felt and encountered. Perhaps my review of my free writing awakened in me what was interesting and exciting to me, so I knew where my happiness was, amidst all those requirements. However, the job market rarely provided me with what I had desired to obtain, which forced me to create a balance between my life and my work, allowing me to search for myself outside my work. This prompted me to search for a permanent and stable feeling in myself, which I found in learning about the esoteric sciences and the history of civilizations, religions, and philosophies in general.

One thing remained, which was how to get rid of the influence of others on me, a trait that originated with me since my youth, and it is about being loved. Therefore, I put a distance between them, so that I have a space for free thinking and not indulge in the attractive aura of others. I was convinced, after a long time, that I cannot please everyone, and that I should not be under anyone's influence, because that would certainly keep me from knowing myself. With my development, I found it difficult to maintain a relationship with many of my friends, because they looked at me as if they were looking at the person they knew years ago, which was not true, and that may have confused them, which led me to drift away from them.

I tried to understand these people, and not to prejudge anyone, if I do not know the situation they are going through, nor the reasons for the problem. Prejudice is considered one of the negative thoughts that destroy integrity and freedom of analysis, while positive thinking develops the self by opening to others and benefiting from their experiences. It will also open a new world, in which we may find our happiness, where we can fulfill our dreams. It may be uncomfortable to get out of our habits, and what we have learned in our lives, but it is necessary to learn new experiences and to better know ourselves, what we love, what we hate, and what we wish for.

My approach to things was questions crossing my mind, and my answers were written down so that time would not erase them. When I imagined that I might have enough money to spend the rest of my life without work, and this only happened during my retirement, I wished to devote my time to writing, and that is what is happening now. Each of us has certain wishes, which may vary or conform with the wishes of others. Some may want to work in the fields, which was one of my dreams that I never realized, whereas some may want to travel or practice painting. What is important is that a person dreams and that his dreams do not stop, because that is how his life ends. Many things happened that I still regret, because I did not make more effort in the past, although that does not work now benefit me now. Changing the past is impossible, and we must only learn the lesson and turn the page. The person I was hoping to be had the qualities of gods and prophets, because I never wished to be a ruler, even if the rulers were the winners. I always wanted to be myself, because I found it impossible to bypass my shadow. So, my question was always: Who am I? I first sought to be my father's son, and a person of value in society, loved and respected by people, but that did not convince me enough, so I tried to go beyond what I had learned, and walk steadily on a path not taken by anyone before. My final answer was, with Father Pierre Teilhard de Chardin: "I am a spirit undergoing an earthly experience and not a body undergoing a spiritual experience". This was the pinnacle of my findings and what I always try to be. I did not live in dreams, but rather in real life. I was not making excuses, but rather I was planning, as far as my knowledge, to overcome obstacles. I always acted according to what I knew. For example, if I planned to travel, I traveled, and everything was easy to reach. However, that was an incentive for me to continue my efforts because I was looking for the unknown within me, and I was not convinced by the goal that I had reached. My life was a journey into the unknown, in which I learned a lot, especially when I encountered obstacles, when I used to fall and start again. However, it was my self-confidence that ignited my feelings and motivated me to do more to know myself. The only thing that bothered me was the dissatisfaction with what I had reached because I wanted to reconcile my soul with my body, and that was not an easy thing; rather, it was impossible. However, being busy helping my family and others was a way to discover myself. My professional knowledge was not exclusive to me; I shared it with my fellow engineers, as I shared my knowledge of life matters with those I approached and asked. My viewing of the hardships experienced by others has made me aware of the true extent of my fears. This helped me see what I enjoy and be grateful for the opportunities I have had in my life. This created a deeper awareness of myself and of my ability to differentiate between what matters in life and what does not. Then emerged the hidden relationship that binds me to the Divine Providence, which I always appreciated, because I felt I spoke on its behalf.

In this intimate atmosphere of spiritual revelations, and after properly meditating on kindness and compassion, I felt that there was no difference between me and the others. My real journey began with the light of a spiritual spectrum that guided me to my real self. I entered my hermitage because I couldn't find a place quieter than my soul. However, when I work with passion, or when I read about a new scientific discovery, or know how much prayer has been useful to a patient's healing, and how pure intentions are recorded in the higher heaven and from there we are showered with blessings and dignities, all of which is comparable to my entry into my hermitage. My quest for the truth is the axis around which my life revolves. It is said that the truth has several aspects, which are relative and are hidden in the symbol. I am searching for the simple truths that enter a person's practical life, which he needs to be happy. This does not mean that my request is only human happiness, but rather the way to discover it and to know the meaning of life and the possibility of his conscious participation in its making. This stems from a certain intention, to know the truth of happiness that leads us to spiritual peace. Moreover, sensing the event through intuition is one of the most important means that connects us to the subconscious mind. Here, my happiness is characterized by the depth of its goals and objectives for the sake of the common good, because I aspire to see humanity evolve through discoveries and revelations of life and spirit. When explained in detail, it is possible to show the stability of its foundations. The events that have occurred so far are only conclusive evidence to show the validity of my convictions. I feel that there is a spiritual process going on behind the scenes of life, and this is what prompts me to reject materialistic concepts. As a result, and according to these concepts, our presence on Earth is limited to a simple struggle for survival. This is synonymous with what is happening today in temples, where prayers are limited to the repetition of phrases that have been used for thousands of years. We also discover the trivial tools and exhibits by the amusement and entertainment factories to quell our anxiety in the face of existence. We wish to live a life full of mysterious coincidences and sudden intuition. Surely, it leads us down the path designated for us here. Each of us must seek to gather information and knowledge because our fate is expected in advance, and only unfolds at the end of a long journey. This type of quest is like a police investigation that occurs within us, and its indicators lead us to progress from one discovery to another. We can live a true inner experience. If we can find the necessary connection, our lives will benefit from a very important flow of spiritual clarity and intuition. Little by little, partial information is being communicated to us about our fate and about the task we can undertake. However, to achieve that, we must liberate ourselves from the habits that convert us from our spiritual path, we must respect some ethical rules in our relationships with others, and remain attentive to our hearts. We must review the myths about the field of prayer. We must understand how the different elements can fit into each other. It all starts with the awareness that the energy of prayer is real, that it flows outside of ourselves and affects the outside world.

In order to increase that energy, we must first improve the quality of energy absorbed by the body. The higher the energy level, the more we realize the beauty of things and creatures.

Then the energy of prayer begins to take effect when we know how to organize this field of prayer to increase the simultaneous flow in our lives. To get that result, we must remain conscious and alert, anticipating new intuitions or coincidences to occur to develop our existence. This expectation releases our energy outside of ourselves, away from it, and makes it more stable, because, from now on, we align our intentions with the programmed process of growth and evolution in the universe.

Then we expect that the field of prayer radiates and intersects with the energy level of others, which prompts them to focus on their inner connection with the Divine and on their intuition with their higher selves. This increases the level of synchronization between us and them.

Finally, we will discover the importance of stabilizing and maintaining the flow of energy despite the state that triggers our fear and anger. We must remain separate from events, search for positive meanings, and believe that the process will save us.

What has been revealed so far will expand to include all the history and culture of humanity. On a certain level, we know that we have come from another dimension, a divine dimension, to participate on earth in a global project: the creation of a completely spiritual civilization on this planet, slowly and generation after generation. However, the moment we acquire this harmonious vision, a new revelation appears to the public: the mystery of transcendental consciousness. Our thoughts and behavior participate in the realization of our dreams. We will eventually understand how our wishes, prayers, and even our beliefs or our secret assumptions affect, at the same time, our personal development and the development of others.

This is based on my personal experience and the investigations of the modern world, and this book seeks to clarify the new phase of our transcendental consciousness. This revelation will emerge mainly in the world, as it is the focus of attention and thousands of discussions. Only hatred and fear, which weigh heavily on our present day, prevent it from appearing to the outside world. We must live in harmony with the knowledge we discover, to understand it well, and to spread the good word.

When we introduce a new concept that does not conform to the existing concepts, we declare a revolution against reality, despite ourselves. Transcendental Consciousness is a non-generalized concept of what the world might one day experience, due to the clarification of the purpose of prayer, intuition, and human relationships that aim at the same vision. We have embraced research that deals with one topic and marginalizes one side to highlight the characteristics of another. I do not like this behavior in research, if it is impossible to explore fully the depths of anything. We see good in evil, beauty in ugliness, honesty in lying, order in chaos, so that we are unable to favor a specific side. Of course, murder is a crime that is punishable by law, and we cannot see virtue in it. However, we cannot know everything surrounding the killer, why he committed his crime, and what his psychological state is. We are called to approach any subject without negatively affecting anyone, to adopt honesty in our feelings, to adopt the scientific methods for scientific subjects, and to use intuition in matters involving religion. Therefore, I will try to build bridges between cultures, discover the common position between them, highlight the positive side in each, and try to modify their vision of the world and existence through their concepts and beliefs. Goodness is present in everything, and so is beauty, and when they are in our purpose of things, our work is successful and fruitful. I came to this life and I found it full of everything, like an orchard in a forest, and I must differentiate between the beautiful and the ugly, the useful and the harmful. I must progress with knowledge and maintain my freedom of choice.

***

20. The Most Dangerous Problems of Planet Earth

The world is witnessing a rapid development in all fields of sciences, which make human well-being and comfort a goal, as well as rapid profit, causing imbalance in our civilization. The human being was able to know the measurement of natural phenomena and their degree of danger. Here are the most dangerous problems on Earth and their inhabitants:

When we illegally consume harmful energy resources, it increases the temperature of the earth and water, causes the melting of ice, causes a rise in the level of water in the oceans, the occurrence of hurricanes, and the extinction of animals and plants. It is the phenomenon of global warming and climate variability.

Our societies have become addicted to petroleum products, such as oil, gas, and coal, and our method of producing and consuming energy is the reason for the rest of the problems that we suffer from.

Seventy per cent (70%) of the land is covered in water, but only 1% is potable. Water means life, and without it, there is no life on Earth. We must monitor the cleanliness of the water so that we have healthy agricultural produce.

The Earth is spoiled by polluting it. There is audio, visual, radioactive, water, and air pollution, which affects our ecosystem and natural balance. Burning fuel and releasing harmful chemicals cause air pollution. In addition, the dumping of solid and organic waste, oil spills, ship and factory waste, and sewage results in water pollution and diseases. Every day, about 26,000 people die because of hunger and water pollution, and this is an imminent danger.

The most draining of human and natural resources are the wars that leave behind human victims, injustice to nature, and invaluable environmental damage. Most of the state's budget goes to wars.

The situation has led us to excessive consumption in general, with more garbage and deterioration in public health. Incorrectly recycling waste causes water and air pollution.

The development of industry and building supplies has assisted in the deforestation and elimination of the lungs of the Blue Planet. According to the UN report, 18 million acres of forest were lost in the previous year, which is about half of tropical forests. These forests help reduce greenhouse gas emissions, which cause global warming, absorb gases and carbon, and produce oxygen and water vapor.

There is over-fishing, which is the daily primary source of protein for more than 1.2 billion people. In addition, for every kilogram of shrimp, 9 kilograms of other huge marine creatures are thrown away, which threatens marine life.

From day to day, we hear about the extinction of animals and plants due to technology and global warming, which causes environmental imbalance and affects human life.

The population of the Earth has tripled in the last 60 years, and this is considered an excessive growth, threatening famine, poverty, and pollution.

As aforementioned, we see the effect of the lack of awareness exhibited through the behavior of bad societies and in the threat to life on the planet, and this is our responsibility.

***

21. The Unity of Prayer and The Sixth Sense

A long time ago, the gods spoke of a courageous project for all humankind and discussed this matter with the knight, who was at the head of the brave, asking him to watch over the world. They inspired him to go to the Lady of the Lake, who presented him with a golden sword, the sword of victory, Excalibur. Thus, the knight advanced on the path of the sun and gathered brave men on the top of the mountain of purity, and began their prayer with a hymn from the Veda: O holy fire! Oh, pure fire! You are the one who sleeps in the forest, and you rise with flame on the altar of the gods, you are the heart of sacrifice, you are the bold ascension of prayer, you are the divine spark hidden in all things, and the spirit of the glorious sun.

Prayer has resonated in the world at lightning speed, and touched my ears like a mass of light, then

I saw it rising towards the full moon, and behold, it leaves its place and disappears into space. There was a commotion on the face of the earth, and I felt that my bones were breaking; maybe I no longer needed them. I remembered that I was on an earthly mission, aspiring to a new world, bringing together the elite of all ages, where their consciousness has evolved to transcend the individual to all humankind. I contemplated carefully on these **visitors**, who are passing by the earth, and they need someone to feed them, educate them, provide them with job opportunities, and ways to communicate. As soon as they enter the arena of life, they will find the paths of religions paved before them; they only must follow, and paradise awaits them. I tried to enter their minds, and I found them locked up with a series of hypotheses. Then time stopped, as if creativity had died in the hearts, and people were programmed to perform their obligatory duties, to be saved from the fire. I paused for a long time when I contemplated these people, who have willingly nailed themselves to the cross of slavery, and I hoped that if the revelation would come to me, I would realize the validity of what I felt. Here, revelation is in the sense of intuition, because my spiritual energies are working in the best way. I have no ambition to change anyone, but rather to be able to see the historical paths of people. I am convinced that things can only develop from within, and humans can only change with consciousness. The problem with religions, which are not based on any scientific principle, is that they assume transcendental consciousness as a form of entering the realm of the jinn. Here, it is difficult for a person to take a single step without being bombarded with accusations that he is working against religion. Therefore, I thought it would be better to contemplate a world that stands as an idol between assumptions that are thousands of years old, and a creative human mind that can push it to the fields of knowledge and development. The world's ignorance of what to do leads it to the serious problems that I mentioned in a previous chapter. Should we leave this world in its ignorance, or remove the obscurity from its eyes that prevent it from seeing clearly? From our starting point, we must set the goal and work to reach it. The world today is sleeping in a dream and walking on the brink of an abyss. My hope is that man awakens from his deep slumber and participates in writing the history of civilization. if we cannot save, fate comes despite us. Perhaps prayer and intuition will help the elite meet in the ether and work on developing a joint project to change the face of the world.

***

22. The Road to Damascus

Acts 9:1-30 New International Version (NIV)

Saul's Conversion

[9 Meanwhile, Saul was still breathing out murderous threats against the Lord's disciples. He went to the high priest [2] and asked him for letters to the synagogues in Damascus, so that if he found any there who belonged to the Way, whether men or women, he might take them as prisoners to Jerusalem. [3] As he neared Damascus on his journey, suddenly a light from heaven flashed around him. [4] He fell to the ground and heard a voice say to him, "Saul, Saul, why do you persecute me?"

[5] "Who are you, Lord?" Saul asked.

"I am Jesus, whom you are persecuting," he replied. [6] "Now get up and go into the city, and you will be told what you must do."

[7] The men traveling with Saul stood there speechless; they heard the sound but did not see

anyone. [8] Saul got up from the ground, but when he opened his eyes, he could see nothing. Therefore, they led him by the hand into Damascus. [9] For three days he was blind, and did not eat or drink anything.

[10] In Damascus, there was a disciple named Ananias. The Lord called to him in a vision, "Ananias!"

"Yes, Lord," he answered.

[11] The Lord told him, "Go to the house of Judas on Straight Street and ask for a man from Tarsus named Saul, for he is praying. [12] In a vision, he has seen a man named Ananias come and place his hands on him to restore his sight."

[13] "Lord," Ananias answered, "I have heard many reports about this man and all the harm he has done to your holy people in Jerusalem. [14] And he has come here with authority from the chief priests to arrest all who call on your name."

[15] But the Lord said to Ananias, "Go! This man is my chosen instrument to proclaim my name to the Gentiles and their kings and the people of Israel. [16] I will show him how much he must suffer for my name."

[17] Then Ananias went to the house and entered it. Placing his hands on Saul, he said, "Brother Saul, the Lord—Jesus, who appeared to you on the road as you were coming here—has sent me so that you may see again and be filled with the Holy Spirit."

[18] Immediately, something like scales fell from Saul's eyes, and he could see again. He got up and was baptized, [19,] and after taking some food, he regained his strength.

Saul in Damascus and Jerusalem

Saul spent several days with the disciples in Damascus. [20] At once, he began to preach in the synagogues that Jesus is the Son of God. [21] All those who heard him were astonished and asked, "Isn't he the man who raised havoc in Jerusalem among those who call on this name? And hasn't he come here to take them as prisoners to the chief priests?" [22] Yet Saul grew more and more powerful and baffled the Jews living in Damascus by proving that Jesus is the Messiah.

[23] After many days had gone by, there was a conspiracy among the Jews to kill him, [24] but Saul learned of their plan. Day and night, they kept close watch on the city gates to kill him. [25] But his followers took him by night and lowered him in a basket through an opening in the wall.

[26] When he came to Jerusalem, he tried to join the disciples, but they were all afraid of him, not believing that he was a disciple. [27] But Barnabas took him and brought him to the apostles. He told them how Saul, on his journey, had seen the Lord and that the Lord had spoken to him, and how in Damascus he had preached fearlessly in the name of Jesus. [28] So Saul stayed with them and moved about freely in Jerusalem, speaking boldly in the name of the Lord.

[29] He talked and debated with the Hellenistic Jews, [a] but they tried to kill him. [30] When the believers learned of this, they took him down to Caesarea and sent him off to Tarsus.

Thus, the weighing trays are equal. It is the balance of Divine Justice that rejects wrongfully on anyone, so how if the injustice be on the Lamb of God! In all matters of our lives, however, we are convinced of the correctness of our thoughts and intransigence, our subconscious mind must intervene and give attention to the voice of conscience, the voice of truth. We must walk the middle path, the path of wisdom between rigor and mercy. I saw it as my duty to place points on the lines of transcendental consciousness, and to carry in my heart the image that I have created, of a world in which we all share, willingly or unwillingly. I have my world and you have yours, and with free will, we must build the foundations of peace, no matter how different our vision of God, the universe, and man is. Religion is a controversial term, concerned with faith or belief associated with the sacred and the divine, as well as morality and practice. Some have defined it as the sum of answers that explain the relationship between humans and the universe. Religions differ across cultures.

There are still tribes in the jungles and forests, unaware of the existence of human civilization, and if anyone manages to go to them, they would say that he came from another world outside the Earth!

There are still people who consider the Earth flat, and deny that it is like a ball swimming in space and revolving around itself and around the sun!

As for the Jewish people, they believe that God has chosen them as His servants and to be how the world. They believe that they can't mix with other people. Moreover, God did not choose them as a people only, but as a religious group united by their ideas and beliefs; and the choice indicates the superiority of the Jewish race. The Jews were chosen because they are descendants of the prophet Abraham, as it says in the Talmud: All Jews are holy, all Jews are princes. Jewish religious tradition mentions that Moses's body was transferred to heaven by angels in honor of him after his death, so that his body would not be corrupted. This is confirmed by the New Testament, knowing that the same has happened in a variety of ways with others, such as Elijah and Christ.

Christianity, or Christendom, is an Abrahamic and monotheistic religion, centered in its teachings around the Bible, and especially Jesus, who is in the doctrine, the fulfiller of the expected prophecies, and who is the incarnate Son of God. Jesus, who presented in the New Testament the climax of spiritual, social, and moral teachings, and who demonstrated His teachings with His miracles, was the savior of the world by His death and His resurrection, and the only intermediary between God and mankind. Most Christians await His second coming, which concludes with the resurrection of the dead, where God will reward the righteous in an eternal kingdom of happiness.". Gate of Religions, Wikipedia

What aroused my attention was what the Apostle Paul said to Peter: "If you, as a Jew, live in a Gentile nation and not a Jew, then why should the nations be converted to Judaism?" This indicates the openness of Christianity to the world.

"The Holy Quran is the main holy book in Islam, which Muslims believe to be a revelation from God (Allah) to the prophet Muhammad, for the statement and the miracles that are frequently transmitted and worshiped in his recitation, and it is the last of the heavenly books after the **Scrolls** of Abraham, the **Zabur**, the **Torah** and the **Gospel**." Gate of Religions. Wikipedia

Hinduism is a word invented by the Western world to incorporate the religious and social system of India. Hinduism or Brahmanism is the dominant religion in India and Nepal. It is a group of beliefs and traditions formed over a long journey from the fifteenth century BC to the present day. One of its direct origins is the historical Vedic religion since the Iron Age of India. Hinduism includes spiritual and moral values, as well as legal and organizational principles, employing several gods according to the actions related to them. Each region has a god, and every action or phenomenon has a god.

Buddhism, named after Gautama Buddha, is considered one of the world's major religions, founded by the teachings left by the "awakened" or "enlightened" Buddha. It originated in northern India and gradually spread throughout Asia. The original doctrine is based on two principles:

1 – The living move during their life cycle, from one life to another, and from one body to another, a person, a god, an animal, an outcast, and so on.

2. The nature of the afterlife is determined according to the deeds accomplished by the living being in their previous life. Those who performed great deeds are rewarded with a better life, while those who performed evil deeds live a miserable and arduous life.

Buddha's teachings can be summed up by the following four noble truths:

1 Suffering

2 The origin of suffering

3 Stop suffering. The state is called Nirvana or spiritual serenity.

4 The way to stop suffering is the right path in everything.

We are before different cultures and religions that share one destiny, but the greater percentage of them live in constant conflict with each other, whose strength is diluted by the enlightened on all sides. The disasters that threaten humans are mostly from the creation of ignorant and slackening man, with his outdated traditions and rigid beliefs. The various interpretations of religious texts, the unregulated and the unbalanced, are the main cause of conflicts, closeness, and exclusion. I am not saying to change the origins of the text, but to re-read them by the development of history and aesthetics, and with everything that would raise humans and their proximity to humanity, which is stolen by ignorance, fanaticism, intolerance, and the policy of control. All religions present in their texts the coming of a Savior outside of humanity, whether Christ in Judaism or the Messiah's second coming in Christianity, or Christ the son of Mary for the Sunnah, or the Coming of Al-

Mahdi for the Shiites. I am not among those who are waiting, even though I respect everyone's beliefs. What is important is that humanity develops with science, education, and culture, the goals set by UNESCO, in the United Nations, after the Universal Declaration of Human Rights. However, the populace still differs in terms of science, education, and culture, as is common in the international community, and they need to accept other cultures. The 21st century has come, and the world has plunged into war once again, with thousands of deaths and people falling victim to violence. We need men of peace who resemble those noble figures who have reached a state of spiritual serenity, such as Mahatma Gandhi, Nelson Mandela, Martin Luther King, the Dalai Lama, and others. Every person convinced that he is born to a conscious mission of renouncing violence and consolidating peace in his society can communicate with the conscious elite by developing his sixth sense and inner powers. The world now needs people who dream big and believe themselves to be the great benefactors of all humanity. Stop clinging to the past, however enlightening it may have been, or how it has helped humankind to progress and thrive, because the institutions that committed themselves to conveying the message have abandoned the essence of the issue: human development towards humanity rather than the frozen, unseen laws and the outdated canons. Let each one of us be the mission of the avatar, who found and was convinced by his mission to bring peace and unity to the world, by ending the war between the nation of fire, the nation of death, wars, and destruction against the three other nations that work to develop humanity, preserve life, and cooperate for the sake of freedom, brotherhood, equality, and peace among people.

Perhaps we need a person like Melchizedek, without a father or mother, who has no beginning of days, and no end of life.

That is, he entered history suddenly, and came out of it suddenly, without knowing for him the beginning of days, nor the end of life … rather, he appeared at a time to deliver a message, and to be a symbol, without knowing his history or his lineage.

The Name of Melchizedek in Hebrew is מ ,לככ ·י- צדדקק and in Greek is εελιισεεκ.

The first time the name of Melchizedek was mentioned was when he received Abraham upon his return from the Kedar el Ahmar "Kedar the Red", a hero in the Arabian Story, of Omer and the kings who were with him (Genesis 18 14-20). In this interview, it was said about Melchizedek what follows:

1 - He is the king of Salem (Jerusalem).

2 - He is a priest of the Highest God and has offered bread and wine.

3 - He blessed Abraham, and Abraham gave him the tithes.

Moreover, Paul the Apostle decides that Melchizedek is greater than Abraham.

Considering that the young is blessed by the old (Heb 7 7). Moreover, considering that he paid him tithes. Thus, the priesthood of Melchizedek is greater than that of Aaron, who was at the heart of Abraham when Melchizedek blessed him.

The priesthood of Christ, and the Christian priesthood, is according to the Melchizedek rite.

***